Reforming Britain: The journey to the centre of British Politics

John R Clarke

Published by:

Book Publication Ltd

Great Portland Street

London W1W 7LT

UK

Dedication

I would like to dedicate this book to my colleagues and friends at Wokingham Reform UK, especially our chairman, John Halsall, who has taught me so much about politics in such a short time. I would also like to mention the Emmbrook ward volunteers and supporters, without whom it would be impossible to make any impact in Emmbrook.

Special dedication to Sam and Kalpna as always.

About the Author

John R Clarke is an Evangelical Christian based in Wokingham, Berkshire, England. He holds a PhD in Medical Virology along with several other postgraduate qualifications. A seasoned writer, he has authored four books, contributed to seven others, and published over 80 papers in peer-reviewed journals. He has worked as a medical writer for five medical communications companies for over 18 years and retired as a Scientific Director Content Specialist in 2022. During his time as a medical writer, he developed extensive expertise in writing peer-reviewed manuscripts, reviews, patient pamphlets, monograms and textbooks.

With over 40 years of experience as a lay preacher and a longstanding interest in public discourse, Dr Clarke brings both academic rigour and personal conviction to his work. He has been a member of Reform UK since 2024.

Contents

Preface

The thoughts and arguments within this book are my own and do not reflect the views of others, and the book has not been endorsed by Reform UK. To understand the role of political parties in the UK today, there is a need to understand what politics is and how it should function and in reality, how it differs from its intended purpose. What we believe we have voted for is not necessarily what we get. The single biggest difficulty we face in Britain today is a total loss of hope, apart from Christians whose lives are shaped by the belief in the resurrection of Jesus and the indication of a new creation; there is very little hope of a better future for the citizens of this country. We declare that Britain is a Christian country, but what do we mean by that, and how does it affect citizens of other religious persuasions? It is clear that, in the original sense of the word, the laws set out in the Bible have largely been adopted in all Western countries.

The impact of political ideology on the needs of the people of Britain, and how ideology impacts key concerns such as uncontrolled immigration. Why immigration is the centre of discontent in the country is analysed and discussed. There is a comparison of how other European countries are dealing with immigration. The impact that the European Court of Justice has on governmental decisions and the power of the courts over the government in terms of what the courts tell us is legal versus illegal, and the impact of these decisions on the British people. This is coupled with the expectation of a better life in Britain and the likelihood of utopia ever being achieved in Britain. The problems of broken promises and constant U-turns by the Labour government, and how their decisions have impacted the British economy and the move towards economic oblivion. The impact and consequences of net zero, the cancellation and reinstatement of local elections, the attempt to muzzle and eliminate free speech in the UK, Labour's attempts to reverse Brexit without a mandate from the people and their policy to enforce identity cards. Labour's support for the prosecution of UK armed forces veterans. The lack of care for the victims of rape gangs, their decision to destroy court records and the fiasco of the Chagos islands are all discussed. Fake news and manipulative reporting of the news are discussed. The rise of Reform UK since 2024, the defections of high-profile figures and the role of grassroot members in the rise of Reform UK. There is a special emphasis on the London Mayoral elections. Nigel Farage has pledged to restore law and order to London in 2026 and emphasised that lawlessness was the predominant issue in London.

What Reform UK are hoping to achieve, their policies and direction. What comes next for Reform UK is the implementation of key policies and core pledges, and the obstacles that need to be overcome. A Reform UK government must deliver on its promises, and there can be no excuses. If elected, we have a mandate to reverse years and years of wastefulness and failure of both the Conservatives and the Labour Governments. What is required to restore justice, British culture and values, and develop British industry after decades of neglect? Dealing with a declining GDP, national debt and restoring international trade. Finally, I have outlined local issues as it impacts on a small town in Berkshire, England. Crime rates, council tax waste, local building plans and the impact of ideology on local businesses and I have provided a personal view of what is missing.

John R Clarke

Chapter 1:

The Nature of Politics

What Is Politics?

Politics consists of all the activities of conflict, negotiation and cooperation over the use and dissemination of assets, whatever place they are found within or beyond formal institutions, on a global level or within a family, involving two or more people. Harold Laswell defined politics as "who gets what, when and how." The ultimate defining purpose of politics is governing and making policy. Governance needs to be understood fundamentally as a provision of direction to the economy and society.[1] Governance is deciding on collective goals for society and then devising the mechanisms through which these goals can be attained.[2] Politics is a relationship between the power and influence of states and their societies. Governance involves setting collective goals for society and reconciling repeated wants and demands within that society.[3] Governance also involves creating capacity for implementing and steering so that the goals that are established through some political processes are made effective and produce the intended changes in the economy and society. Coherence inevitably.

There are numerous institutions involved in governance, and it follows, therefore, that there will be numerous policy priorities and

---

[1] Guy Peters, Politics is about governing, page 24. In What is politics? Edited by Adrian Leftwich. Polity Press, Cambridge, UK 2004
[2] Peters, page 25
[3] Peters, page 26

preferences.[4] The need to coordinate can be most clearly seen in public bureaucracy, where the various ministries and agencies created to deliver public programmes all believe that their goals are the most important and therefore other organisations should bow to their wishes.[5] There needs to be a mechanism for detecting and assessing the actions of the governance system.[6] There are a number of diverse interests in society, and many of those interests are able to influence governments sufficiently to have programmes developed for their benefit. The ultimate aspect of politics is assessment and accountability.[7]

What is to be counted politically? What is the nature of or characteristic feature of politics?[8] To define politics in terms of conflict is not enough. We need further criteria to tell us which conflicts are political.[9] What is distinctive about politics and occurs in all cases of politics is a class of laws solely concerned with securing the position of the state and the government; laws covering treason, subversion, opposition, criticism, loyalty, and official secrets all come into play.[10] There are also laws that provide services for members of society to do with health, housing, employment, transport, energy, education and so on. We cannot avoid politics, and it may involve being forced to do things or pay for things we may not wish to.[11]

Politics is about matters such as censoring, entertainment, allowing women to have abortions, controlling the use of drugs and alcohol,

---

[4] Peters, page 26
[5] Peters, page 26
[6] Peters, page 27
[7] Peters, page 31-33
[8] Peter P Nicholson, Politics and the exercise of force, Page 41. In What is politics? Edited by Adrian Leftwich. Polity Press, Cambridge, UK 2004
[9] Nicholson, page 44
[10] Nicholson, page 45-46
[11] Nicholson, page 46

overseeing the adoption of children, regulating scientific experiments, permitting the practise of religions, permitting the building of a certain type of power station, overseeing arms deals, giving overseas aid, joining international organisations, and going to war with other states.[12]

The Biggest Problem Challenging Britain Today

The single biggest difficulty we face in Britain today is a total loss of hope, apart from Christians whose lives are shaped by the belief in the resurrection of Jesus and the indication of a new creation; there is very little hope of a better future for the citizens of this country.[13] Despite earlier hope, science and technology are seen as threats rather than a way to a better life.[14] Despite the conquering of nearly all of the deadly pestilences of previous generations and the overcoming of COVID in recent years, the burden on health services in all Western nations is exceeding available resources.[15] Modern ideologies have urged citizens to abandon their trust in God and embrace a manmade utopia on earth, but these have largely been dismissed by the mass of the population as successive Governments have failed to deliver on their promises of a better life.[16]

The question now is whether our present critique of our country is a healthy questioning or whether our culture is nearing its death.[17] Until recently, there was hope that there must at least in principle be a

---

[12]Nicholson, page 46

[13] Lesslie Newbigin. The other side of 1984, page 1. World Council of Churches, Geneva, Switzerland.1990 edition.

[14] Newbigin, page 2.

[15] Newbigin, page 2.

[16] Newbigin, page 3.

[17] Newbigin, page 3.

solution to the country's problems, but we are coming to terms with the reality that there are problems in life for which there are no solutions.[18] Therefore, do we need to develop new models for dealing with the human condition within Western countries?[19]

A Christian Country

We declare that Britain is a Christian country, but what do we mean by that, and how does it affect citizens of other religious persuasions? It is clear that in the original sense of the word, the laws set out in the Bible have largely been adopted in all Western countries, thou shalt not kill, murder is punished by imprisonment. Thou shalt not steal, theft is also deemed to be punishable by either a hefty fine or a prison sentence, depending on the extent of the theft, but more recently by who the judge is and sadly also by who the thief is. However, most Western countries no longer hold the punishment of crime to the same severity as the Bible. For example, rape in Deuteronomy 22:25-27 was punishable by death, while currently in the UK, some Muslims found guilty of rape are given token prison sentences, some as little as 12 months. Personally, I would advocate that the death sentence be reintroduced for everyone who rapes a child. The question that needs to be addressed for the UK and most Western countries is "Does Christianity have a vision for society as a whole?"[20] Or put another way, "Should Christians have a vision for society, for the state, for politics?"[21] A further consideration is to understand that the purpose of government should be to bless everyone under its care and authority and not to manipulate governmental authority in a way that is

---

[18] Newbigin, page 18.
[19] Newbigin, page 18.
[20] Mark Dever. God and politics, page 1. 10 publishing, Leyland, UK. 2016.
[21] Dever, page 16.

advantageous to the government at the expense of its citizens.[22] It is clear that if a country is to maintain its Christian principles, then all those in government are called to uphold and reflect on the morality that God has created, and the government should reflect God's character and purpose as laid down in the Bible.[23] The downside to this direction is that the majority of our current government is, at best, atheist or, at worse of communist persuasion or ideology. Therefore, they do not see themselves bound to the precepts of a Christian country and follow the belief that "religion is the opium of the people." It is worth noting that in 1843, when Marx made his original observation that opium was legal and was a common medicine, it was also an addictive drug with calming and hallucinogenic properties.[24] Marx's comments no doubt resonate with members of the Fabian Society, of whom most Labour MPs are signed-up members.

The European Union constitution is humanistic and declares that in a multifaith society, Christian precepts cannot be the custom or foundations of the law.[25] Consequentially, evangelical Christians are considered a 'sect,' and any group that does not belong to the Roman Catholic church are castigated and viewed with caution. There have been reports of persecution of Protestant Christians across Europe, including in Germany, Greece, Austria, Belgium, and subsequently in the UK, where Christians have been arrested for street preaching while Muslims are allowed to preach what would amount to hate speech unchallenged.[26] Currently, the Labour government is considering a draft definition of anti-Muslim hatred which does not include the term

---

[22] Dever, page 21.
[23] Dever, page 25.
[24] Esther Oluffa Pedersen. Religion is the opium of the people: An investigation into the intellectual context of Marx's critique of religion. History of political thought 2015; 36:354-387 (page 357)
[25] Hilton. Page119.
[26] Hilton. Page119-121.

"Islamophobia."[27] Lord Toby Young is quoted as saying, "Granting Muslims additional protections not extended to people of other faiths will have the effect of increasing anti-Muslim hostility, not reducing it."[28] The Free Speech Union is concerned that any definition of anti-Muslim hatred could infringe on free speech and possibly introduce a blasphemy law through the back door at the exclusion of the rights of other religions.[29] The Labour government is doing its utmost to erode the Christian basis of the country, and only Reform UK is challenging this erosion, and it is good to be a part of the Reform Christian Fellowship group recently set up by Bob Park. Reform is the only political party in the UK which encompasses a specific Christian group. Outside of politics, the sad reality, as Hilton distinctly points out, is that Christians in pursuit of unity, peace and compromise have chosen to ignore the threat of the dissolution of the UK's Christian foundations, principles and traditions.[30] It is refreshing that Nigel Farage has been consistent in declaring that the UK is fundamentally a Christian nation, and this should be acknowledged at all levels of government. Nigel has also recognised that Judeo-Christian beliefs are the roots of everything that is Britain and that if Christian beliefs are valued, then everything will emanate from that belief.[31] On these foundations, Reform UK has openly welcomed members from other religions, such as Muslims, including Zia Yusef and Laila Cunningham, who have made wonderful and valuable contributions to the popularity and values of Reform UK. It was Nigel's declarations and Zia's profound social media posts that attracted me to Reform UK, and ultimately, why I became a member. As Zia has stated, the only thing

---

[27] Christina McSorley. Ministers finalising definition of anti-Muslim hatred. BBC News 15 December 2025
[28] McSorley.
[29] McSorley.
[30] Hilton, page 131.
[31] Campbell Cambell Jack. How Christian is Reform UK? Issachar People. 19 May 2025.

that will work in Britain is not multiculturalism but one culture, one set of rules under one flag.

We accept that there is a legitimate purpose for governments, but all governments are fallible and may introduce laws that are incompatible with the Bible or, at worse are immoral. Therefore, there is a place for civil disobedience and challenge to any government that seeks to introduce statutes that are morally wrong.[32]

We acknowledge that there are Marxist, Muslim and secular utopian visions for the UK, but utopian visions of political systems always lead to tragedy, tyranny and despotism and terrible distortions of God's will.[33]

The Moral Dilemma

Before we can engage in making moral decisions, we need to grasp the conditions that influence our decision-making.[34] What factors in our world influence people's morality?[35] Modern life impacts our every decision and influences the direction our life moves in.[36] It is common that we feel lost, alone and alienated in the current fast-moving world.[37]

Local and national governments are populated by people who appear to inhabit a different world than the one that most people live in. They are blind to the complexities and realities of everyday living.[38] Taxes are randomly imposed on the population, while salaries are frozen and the population struggles to make ends meet in an environment of rising

---

[32] Dever, page 39-40.
[33] Dever, page 55.
[34] David Cook. The moral maze. 1. The world in which we live. Page 1. SPCK London, UK 1983
[35] Cook, page 1.
[36] Cook, page 1
[37] Cook, page 2
[38] Cook, page 3

food prices and utility bills.[39] We don't find it difficult to imagine the end of the world in one massive nuclear war, but we struggle to accept the picture laid out for us in the book of Revelation.[40]

The big questions of modern society are really old questions that revolve around who we are. Why are we here? And where are we heading?[41] Relativism denies that there are any absolutes at all, but it is in conflict with the Bible, which states that you can know the truth and the truth will set you free.[42]

We claim to be a Christian country, but the number of people identifying as Christian has fallen dramatically. In the 2001 census, 71.6% of respondents put Christian as their faith; this had fallen to 46.2% by 2021, and I strongly suspect that the percentage will have fallen much further by the time of the 2031 census. I also suspect that the number of people identifying as Muslim will have greatly increased by the time of the 2031 census. In 2001, only 2.7% of respondents identified as Muslim, which had risen to 6.5% by 2021.[43] It is important to identify the reasons for change, as religion is set to be an important factor for the future of our country.

In the face of alienation and an attempt by modern men to escape into the future, religion has been left behind and, in some cases, discarded.[44] Historically, the Christian faith has focused on the future transformation of the world into a new heaven and new earth free from evil and wickedness.[45] Sadly, this future hope has not compensated for

---

[39] Cook, page 3
[40] Cook, page 4
[41] Cook, page 4
[42] Cook, page 11
[43] Office of National Statistics. Census results 2001 and 2021.
[44] Cook, page 13.
[45] Cook, page 13.

the present reality of suffering and injustice experienced by the majority of people across the world.[46]

The church has consistently failed to address the developments of science, the growth of the industrial nations and the change from rural communities into an urbanised jungle.[47] The church and Christians have lost their moral compass and have not upheld the Biblical teaching on homosexuality, divorce and remarriage, euthanasia, assisted suicide and abortion up to the full gestation of 40 weeks.[48] The moral diversity among Christians is equally met by doctrinal diversity, and relativism has muddied the waters further by insisting that the Bible was written solely for a people of a specific historical epoch and has no relevance for modern man.[49]

Does the modern world have any moral values at all?[50] If there are morals, which aspect of life is the source of morality?[51] Does our ability to reason and to think set us apart as creatures that have morality? Among philosophers, Plato attempted to base our ability to reason as the foundation of his belief system.[52]

Naturalism argues that morality can be discerned by studying the natural world.[53] Good and evil are natural features of the world we live in, but can these be discerned apart from God? For it is written that since the creation of the world God's invisible qualities of His divine nature have been visible to see through His creation (Romans 1:20). Therefore, it is plausible for us to be able to perceive good and evil,

---

[46] Cook, page 13.
[47] Cook, page 15.
[48] Cook, page 15.
[49] Cook, page 16.
[50] Cook, page 18.
[51] Cook, page 20.
[52] Cook, page 21.
[53] Cook, page 23.

right from wrong, from the natural world.[54] However, naturalism becomes difficult when we consider what the natural world meant for 1st century people compared with 21st century modern man.[55] However, since the enlightenment science has replaced God as the new normal by which we should test everything. Therefore, there is now no God whose commandments must be obeyed.[56] Human reason has replaced the doctrines of Biblical reasoning instituted by God, and the dogma of original sin is considered as wicked slander against human reasoning.[57] The largest impact on the world over the last century must come from advances in science and medicine.[58]

Christians are not immune to the impact of the world around us, nor to the values that bombard us each day.[59] The moral dilemma for most Christians is that we live a schizophrenic existence in the 21st century. Christians live in the modern world and are affected by the world around them, and are influenced by the values that surround them.[60] The dilemma for many Christians is that we do not recognise the difference between spiritual values and secular values.[61] In many areas, secular values have both eroded and replaced Christian values without Christians noticing what has occurred.[62]

Creation is taken as a source of Christian moral principles.[63] The Biblical view of Christian ethics relies upon the Holy Spirit living in our hearts and guiding us into all truth (John 16:13).[64] The Holy Spirit calls Christians to be in the world but not of the world, to not follow

---

[54] Cook, page 24.
[55] Cook, page 26.
[56] Newbigin, page 12
[57] Newbigin, page 12
[58] Cook, page 37.
[59] Cook, page 41.
[60] Cook, page 42.
[61] Cook, page 43.
[62] Cook, page 43.
[63] Cook, page 50.
[64] Cook, page 60.

the ways of the world but to be transformed into God's ways by the regenerating of our intellects (Romans 12:2). transformation brings with it a metamorphic change from racing after the things the world values, such as riches and success, to being content with what we have and relying on God to provide our every need. In other words, do not love the world more than our relationship with God (1 John 2:15-19). We should be different and manifest the spiritual characteristics that reflect those of Christ in us. How are Christians to apply spiritual values to the decision-making of everyday living in the modern world?[65]

Faith is not the last thing on the agenda of life, but rather the starting point by which all other experiences of life are to be measured.[66] We must be careful not to descend into legalism, which would argue that we should keep Biblical rules because God has shown us the rules, and we struggle to keep the rules in our vanity to please God or out of fear that we will be punished by God if we fail to keep to the rule book.[67] Christian love is at the centre of Christian morality, and we must seek to implement and impose Christian love on an unsuspecting and ungrateful world if we have any hope of changing the decline of the nation into lawlessness.[68]

According to Danny Kruger, a happy society is an association of people with something in common, something outside of themselves, as individuals, a society of self-determining, self-moralising individuals. It is where the only thing held in common is humanity itself.[69] The idea here is that you are what you worship. No one admits that the enemy

---

[65] Cook, page 63.
[66] Newbigin, page 24.
[67] Cook, page 68
[68] Cook, page 73.
[69] Danny Kruger. The new politics of home, neighbourhood and nation, page 42. Forum Books, Corbridge, UK. 2024

is other people, or proudly declares their wish to subjugate everyone else to their own absolutist worldview. The principle of personal dignity and individual value becomes, I don't care what other people think.[70] However, the problem in the political establishment, driven by short-term popularity, drifting on prevailing winds of fashionable commentary, the real deep-rooted issues in our society and our world are considered too intractable to be tackled.[71]

The Reality of Ideology

The current Labour government has thrown all their manifesto promises into the mud in an attempt to impose a communist regime that aims to keep them in power for decades. At what point in the process does ideology replace common sense, and what is the end game of imposing ideology on the general population? The error of politicians today is that because they have been elected with a majority, they can impose whatever they like, even if it means consistently lying to the electorate about what they are doing. The flaw in their approach is that they think that people are stupid and will not oppose the legislation, no matter the cost, but people will rebel when their way of life is being threatened, and the outcome in most instances will lead to violence on an unprecedented scale.

Immigration on the scale we have seen in the past 20 years has added seven million people to the population between 2000 and 2020, and this is catastrophic for British workers, as GDP per head has not improved but has reduced due to the importation of low-wage workers. This is bad for our economy in general, as this applies to cheap labour, which does away with the need to invest in the

---

[70] Kruger, page 42--43
[71] Liz Truss. Page 16. In Ten Years to save the west. Biteback Publishing, Hull, UK, 2024.

underlying factors of growth, technological innovation and investment in the skills and wellbeing of the people. It's bad for many British places, which have changed quickly and irrevocably.[72] Given the degree of central control of the local government, it is perhaps little wonder that councils hold what power they have and that political cliques dominate local government, to the exclusion of most ordinary people.[73]

I've joined Reform UK, and instantaneously, I have gone from being a decent guy to being a racist, a far-right nut job that should be certified. The insults arising from the left wing of British politics keep flowing and never cease to amaze at the stupidity of some of them. For example, David Lammy's comment that Nigel Farage flirted with the Hitler Youth and the false allegations by school colleagues 50 years ago.[74] It shows that labour and the labour-supporting media are desperate to try to stop the rise of Reform UK because they can't achieve any success through legitimate means.

The fact that I am married to a woman of Indian descent and that for over 40 years I have worked impartially with a wide array of people, some who were Muslim, Hindu, atheist, some who were from Iran, Iraq, Saudi Arabia, Lebanon, Bangladesh, the USA, Bermuda, as well as Scotland and England. It doesn't matter, as soon as you join Reform, you are classed as a fascist and a racist and as David Lammy would have us believe, a product of the Hitler Youth. What a perception and total nonsense, especially as more and more people join Reform, and at the time of writing, Reform is the fastest-growing and largest political party in the UK. Yet, people like Laila Cunningham, who is a

---

[72] Kruger. page 115.

[73] Kruger, page 137.

[74] David Wilcock, Greg Heffer, James Tapsfield. Lammy's grovelling apology. Daily Mail online. 1 October 2025. Sky News. Nigel Farage sang antisemitic songs to Jewish classmates, former Dulwich pupil claims. 6 December 2025.

Muslim and has been selected as Reform's UK party London mayoral candidate, state that she would never join a racist party, and that is a sentiment underlined by many Reform supporters such as Zia Yusef.[75]

There has been a frequent Facebook post in 2025 that defines the far right as people who are in full-time employment (not me I'm retired), they are literate (well I have a PhD and have published four books and written over 80 articles in peer reviewed journals as well as over 100 papers as a medical writer, so there is some hope that I qualify here), thirdly they love their families (I believe I can claim this definition), they administer a lot of common sense (I think my colleagues would agree I qualify here, at least that is what they say to my face) and finally they obey the laws of the land (I have never been arrested or cautioned so I claim this definition for myself).

The overuse of "far right" has desensitised the public, eroding its ability to flag extremist threats. When Reform UK voters are labelled "far right" alongside banned groups like National Action, the term loses its potency. A 2024 YouGov poll showed 55% of British people distrust media labels, reflecting cynicism fuelled by hyperbole. On X, users make fun of The Guardian for imprinting orthodox beliefs as extremist, contending that it trivialises actual neo-Nazis.[76]

Why Reform UK? Because it is the job of political leaders to lead, and those leaders need to have the courage to put our country first and the Reform UK policy that British people will come first under a Reform UK government, is both reassuring and comforting in a country where the labour government puts the rights of immigrants above the rights of the British people.

---

[75] Claudia Cockerill. Reform's Laila Cunningham: 'I would never be a part of a racist party' Evening Standard 16 January 2026.

[76] Common Sense Is Dead Jun 05, 2025. https:// deadcommonsense.substack.com/p/when-everyones-far-right-how-a-loaded

Chapter 2:

Immigration: The Centre of Discontent in The UK

There is no doubt that Britain is broken and is in urgent need of being fixed. As Reform UK is the only political party to acknowledge the brokenness of Britain, the question arises: what is attracting so many people to Reform? Obviously, opinion polls place the uncontrolled influx of migrants and what are termed illegal immigrants persistently come out as the number one reason why people are joining Reform. When labour tells us that they will stop illegal migration, but then have to admit there are thousands of migrants in this country whose whereabouts the government do not know. The government then signs a deal with the EU that will allow even more migrants into Britain. Then it is clear that there is a catastrophe in the making.

If anyone who opposes illegal immigration is called a racist, we should define racism as the understanding that people's attributes are dictated by their ethnicity and that the members of other ethnic groups are not as good as the members of your own, or the resulting unfair treatment of members of other races. It is used in the sense by the communist left in an attempt to alienate people and cause hatred. The people in Reform UK that I know are not racist but are concerned about the unvetted influx of illegal immigrants into our country, which is seriously impacting the traditional values of the British people. What concerns me is those people who come to our country with the view of overthrowing our democracy and way of life in order to impose their Sharia law values on us. I strongly believe such people should be shown the exit door and led out of our country. Giorgia Meloni, the prime minister of Italy, has stated that Islamic views are not compatible with Western values, or European values, and that is something I agree with. Giorgia Meloni has also stated that if you choose to live in a foreign country, you must accept its laws, respect its culture and its traditions.

Immigration continues to be the most alienating political factor across Europe. Even though a number of countries advocate open borders and altruistic migrant policies, others have implemented a firm stance against mass immigration—citing cultural preservation, national security, economic strain, or political stability.[77]

As of November 2025

European Countries Restricting Immigration[78]

The following European countries are known for their restrictive im migration policies:

- **Hungary**: Under Prime Minister Viktor Orban, Hungary has effe ctively abandoned the consideration of asylum applications, retur ning refugees to Serbia or other EU countries. Hungary,   under Prime Minister Viktor Orbán, has become one of Europe's most vocal opponents of immigration. The country implemented fences around their borders to prevent influxes of migrants and implemented inherent modifications that reduce asylum seekers.

---

[77] National Insider November 11, 2025. https:// nationalinsider.co.uk/european-countries-that-do-not-support-immigration-a-closer-look/

[78] Which European Countries Are Tightening Residency Rules in 2025? https:// internationalinvestment.biz/en/observers/5662-which-european-countries-are-tightening-residency-rules-in-2025.html

Orbán's government promotes a nationalist message that emphasises "Christian identity" and national sovereignty.[79]

- **Poland**: Poland has forcibly returned migrants from the border with Belarus and passed a law that allows the right to asylum to be ignored in certain cases. While Poland has accepted large numbers of Ukrainian refugees, it has been resistant to accepting migrants from the Middle East and Africa. Polish leaders believe that forced European Union asylum quotas endanger national unity and societal values. Public support for tighter immigration rules remains high.

- **Finland**: Finland has passed a controversial law that allows refusing entry to refugees from Russia, considering migration an element of a hybrid threat.

- **Germany**: German border police have been ordered to refuse to accept new asylum applications, except in cases of extreme necessity.

- **Austria**: Austria has temporarily suspended the rule on family reunification and supports strict vetting procedures and faster deportations for failed asylum seekers. Austria has oscillated between moderate and hardline positions, especially during election seasons. Conservative parties have pushed for powerful border controls and have connected immigration to national security concerns. The country supports strict vetting procedures and faster deportations for failed asylum seekers.

- **Slovakia:** Slovakia has also opposed mandatory EU migrant redistribution quotas. The government has expressed concern over

---

[79] National Insider and Which European Countries are tightening rules

preserving national identity and has emphasised accepting only Christian refugees, sparking controversy and debate over its selective policies.

- **Italy:** Italy has experienced large-scale migration due to its Mediterranean geography. While national beliefs are divided, there is widespread anti-immigration sentiment, especially concerning asylum seekers arriving by sea. The focal point has been on reducing illegal migration and strengthening asylum policies.

- **Denmark:** Denmark, while known for its strong welfare system, has adopted some of Europe's strictest immigration laws in recent years. This includes measures to seize migrants' valuables, limit non-Western immigration, and incentivise repatriation. Even left-wing political groups have supported stronger immigration laws.

These countries are part of a broader trend in Europe where political pressure, public dissatisfaction and right-wing party influence are leading to more restrictive

immigration policies.

Thoughts From The National Insider States[80]

Not all opposition to immigration in Europe is identical—some countries resist asylum quotas, while others implement laws to curb welfare use or limit cultural integration. What unites these governments is a desire to prioritise national identity, control migration flows, and respond to domestic political pressures. As worldwide immigration continues to mould societies and economies, immigration

---

[80] National Insider November 11, 2025. https:// nationalinsider.co.uk/european-countries-that-do-not-support-immigration-a-closer-look/

will continue to be a defining issue in European politics for years to come.

Certainly, inside Britain, immigration is a daily news item as of November 2025. In their Best for Britain survey conducted between 5 – 10 September 2025, when asked: "Which of the following, if any, do you think are the MOST important issues facing the UK at this time?" The number one concern of those in the survey (4368 adults over the age of 18 years), according to YouGov surveys, 52% of those surveyed placed immigration as the number 1 concern, this compared with 50% who put cost of living, 35% the economy, 25% health and 17% crime.[81]

Why are British people so concerned about immigration? In part, it is mainly concerned with the rapidly changing demographics of the country, such as surveys that show that white Britons were the minority in 23 out of 33 London boroughs.[82] Throughout the 1960s onwards, opinion polls showed that the British people massively opposed the immigration policies of the Westminster government.[83] Tony Blair was the Prime Minister who changed the immigration policy beyond all recognition because they wanted to increase the number of voters who would subsequently be loyal to Labour.[84] During Blair's tenure as Prime Minister, all asylum seekers would be permitted to remain in the UK regardless of whether their claims were authentic or bogus. What the Blair government hadn't realised was that they had catastrophically underestimated the massive influx of

---

[81] YouGov / Best for Britain Survey Results. https://
d3nkl3psvxxpe9.cloudfront.net/documents/BestForBritain_ConferencePolling_September2025_Tables
_W2.pdf
[82] Douglas Murray, page 11-13 in The strange death of Europe: Immigration, Identity and Islam.
Bloomsbury Continuum, London, UK 2018.
[83] Murray, page 15
[84] Murray, page 19

migrants and asylum seekers.[85] Under the Conservative Lib Dem coalition and the subsequent outright Conservative governments, net immigration incessantly rose to approximately 330,000 per year.[86]

In the 12-month period up to June 2025, there were a record 111,084 asylum applications, up 14.4% on the previous year.[87] Hotel accommodation for migrants increased by 2,500 in the first year of the Labour government in comparison with other European nations, where illegal entries have been reduced by half.[88]

It is worth mentioning, considering that Britain is claiming to be a Christian country, going back a few years to before the current predicament of migrations. The 2001 UK census and the 2011 UK census revealed that the number of people living in England and Wales born overseas had risen by 3 million.

The number of Christians had dropped from 72% in 2001 to 59% in 2011. The number of Christians fell from 37 million to 33 million, and the number of Muslims rose from 1.5 million to 2.7 million. However, these numbers did not include the estimated 1 million Muslims who were in the country illegally. White Britons were the minority in 23 out of 33 London boroughs.[89] Throughout the 1960s onwards, opinion polls showed that the British people massively opposed the immigration policies of the Westminster government.[90] Tony Blair was the Prime Minister who changed the immigration policy beyond all recognition because they wanted to increase the number of voters who would subsequently be loyal to Labour.[91] During Blair's tenure as

---

[85] Murray, page 21
[86] Murray, page 22
[87] McCowan, page 53.
[88] McCowan, page 54.
[89] Murray, pages 11-13.
[90] Murray, page 15.
[91] Murray, page 19.

Prime Minister, all asylum seekers would be permitted to remain in the UK regardless of whether their claims were authentic or bogus. What the Blair government hadn't realised was that they had catastrophically underestimated the massive influx of migrants and asylum seekers.[92]

The European Court of Justice

The principles of democracy are eroded by a European autocracy where the principal powers of sovereignty and government are in the hands of a small group of EU bureaucrats.[93] The EU juggernaut has very little to do with democracy but everything to do with power and control.[94] Closer ties with the EU come at a cost to national sovereignty, and decisions are determined by a relatively few people who are not democratically elected as the government of Europe. The most frightening point is that neither the democratically elected European parliament nor national governments can overturn the decisions made by the autocrats.[95] The most intimidating and outlandish of all the European institutions is the European Court of Justice, which has the final say on all questions relating to European Law. In practise, the judges assigned to this court are an amalgamation of former judges, professors of law, private practice lawyers and government advisors.[96] Many of these individuals would not meet the basic standards required to participate in the UK courts of law. It is not the democracy that is failing the citizens of Europe, but the decadent systems that hide in the shadows of the EU.[97] The EU has not suspended democracy; it has dissolved it.[98] The ECHR has taken

---

[92] Murray, page 21

[93] Adrian Hilton. Page 96 In The principality and power of Europe. Dorchester House Publications, Rickmansworth, UK. 2000.

[94] Hilton, page 97.

[95] Hilton, page 98.

[96] Hilton, page 98.

[97] Hilton, page 99.

[98] Hilton, page 101.

away the sovereignty of parliament and has placed democracy, civil liberty and national assets in the hands of the European Court of Justice.[99] History proves that whether dictators like Napolean or, Hitler, or Putin, the creation of an enlarged European Empire across national boundaries will increase the opportunities for the tyrannical abuse of power.[100] The ECHR is not something to be embraced but rather to be feared because justice has moved outside the realms of the British law courts into the whimsical discretion of foreign lawyers.

This can be characterised by the European Court of Justice judgement that Hungary had violated EU laws by forcing asylum seekers to travel to Belgrade or Kyiv in order to obtain travel permits to enter Hungary. The European Court of Justice issued a fine of €200 million.[101] The court will also issue a penalty of €1m a day until it changes its policy. In response, Hungary's Prime Minister Viktor Orbán, in a post on X, said the fine for "defending the borders of the European Union" was "outrageous and unacceptable" and said, "it seems that illegal migrants are more important to the Brussels bureaucrats than their own European citizens." Under EU individuals fleeing persecution in their home country have the right to international protection, and cannot be removed to their home if there is a serious risk of death or torture.[102] This section of EU law has led to the protection from deportation of murderers, paedophiles and rapists from Britain because their crimes would result in the death penalty in their country of origin.

Hungary declined to pay the fine imposed on it by the EU; however, the EU clawed back hundreds of millions of euros by stopping funds earmarked for Hungary after it refused to pay the original fine for

---

[99] Hilton, page 102.
[100] Hilton, page 102.
[101] Mallory Moench. EU court fines Hungary €200m over its asylum policy. BBC News. 13 June 2024.
[102] Moench.

breaking EU asylum laws.[103] A further example of the ECJ's power can be seen in its overruling of the way the Italian government currently defines whether a country is "safe" to return someone whose application is rejected, as this contravenes EU law. That "safe country" concept is central to the deal that Prime Minister Giorgia Meloni struck with Albania in 2023 to send migrants intercepted at sea to Albania for accelerated processing.[104] Italy's prime minister Giorgia Meloni reacted angrily to the ruling because she believed the European Court was encroaching on its role as the ruling weakens the ability of countries to defend their national borders. This highlights the obstacle that the Reform UK government will face in achieving its deportation goals for illegal immigrants and further emphasises the necessity to revoke our membership of the ECHR.

Matters of Life and Death

Two of the most visible areas of moral debate are focused on abortion and assisted dying or euthanasia.[105] Both these area are at the opposite end of life with abortion preventing the beginning of life for the child and assisted dying being at the end of life by an early termination of what for many is a nightmare of deteriorating health often with profound pain and this brings back into the realm of moral dilemma and the discussions in both the House of Commons and the House of Lords show how difficult and complicated an assisted dying law is due to trying to place safeguards that cannot be manipulated. Especially if the person seeking assisted dying is not in a position to sign an agreement, which therefore may fall to an ageing family member.

---

[103] Lorne Cook. Hungary refuses to pay fines for breaking EU asylum rules. Brussels is taking the money anyway. AP News. 18 September 2024.
[104] Sarah Rainsford. Italy plan to process migrants in Albania dealt blow by EU court. BBC News. 1 August 2025.
[105] O'Brien page 86.

Utopia

Another area for consideration concerns our vision of the future. What are we hoping for from our government? Surely any hope of an earthly utopia has long since vanished.[106] The resurrection of Jesus and the free gift of the Holy Spirit are a pledge and foretaste of the victory which will lead to every man bowing down to Jesus as Lord and Saviour of the Cosmos, not just the earth.[107] Therefore, Christians are not seeking an earthly utopia, but the heavenly city which comes down from heaven and which is the home of those who are found written in God's book of life, which is all part of God's new creation.[108]

Christian belief in participating in the risen life and following Him, both by taking up the cross to follow Him and by being a new creation, leaving the old life behind, is not an interior spiritual journey, nor does it lead to creating a new political order.[109] Rather, it should lead us right into the centre of the world's politics and business.[110] It calls into existence the very things that don't exist and looks to support all social and material groups of society, not just the rich but also the poor. This is far removed from the socialist belief, which focuses on a latter-day Robin Hood approach of robbing the rich to support the poor. It also calls into reality responsible spending and investment of taxpayers' money, which is not based on flawed ideology. As Margaret Thatcher declared, *"We know that there is no such thing as public money – there is only taxpayers' money."*[111]

---

[106] Newbigin, page 59

[107] Newbigin, page 34.

[108] Newbigin, page 35.

[109] Newbigin, page 37.

[110] Newbigin, page 37.

[111] Mrs Thatcher, speech to Conservative Party Conference, October, 1983.available at: https://primeeconomics.org/articles/was-375-bn-of-qe-raised-from-taxpayers-is-there-no-such-thing-as-public-money-only-taxpayers-money-as-pm-asserts/

In 2024, when Reform UK's Nigel Farage was labelled "far right" by the BBC for championing tighter immigration controls, many Brits raised an eyebrow. A decade ago, that term conjured images of swastika-toting skinheads or fringe militias, not a suit-clad populist polling double digits. Yet today, from MPs like Lee Anderson to Net Zero Watch campaigners, the "far right" label is slapped on anyone challenging the political mainstream. In a polarised Britain, where Brexit debates still simmer and 55% of Brits distrust media labels (2024 YouGov poll), this once-precise term has become a blunt weapon, diluted to near meaninglessness. How did we get here, and what does it mean for our political discourse?[112]

In search of utopia on earth, Vernon Lee states that he does not feel certain that history or economic theory has proven that intelligence can be forced or emaciated out of existence.[113] Intelligence aims to teach us the most important and essential fact regarding reality, which is otherness, that which is outside of us, that which only God provides. Rather than looking inside ourselves, real intelligence exists beyond what can be comprehended by science, metaphysics, economics, and history, but can only be found by experiencing God.[114] Maybe this is what the Labour Government is missing: any form of intelligence as they bludgeon their way to oblivion.

It is important to note that many ideologies long for utopia on earth, but these ideologies aim to achieve utopia by suppressing the free will of the people. The most notorious of these ideologies was described in George Orwell's book 1984. The classic terminology in 1984 is that Big Brother is Watching You, and nothing can be carried out without

---

[112] Common Sense Is Dead Jun 05, 2025. https:// deadcommonsense.substack.com/p/when-everyones-far-right-how-a-loaded
[113] Vernon Lee. Proteus or the future of intelligence, page 3. Word Wise Publishing, 2024
[114] Lee, pages 18-19.

a citizen being watched with horrific consequences if one strays from the path laid out by Big Brother.[115] Many today have parallel beliefs to those in 1984 that the digital identity that the Labour government wants to impose will lead to a totalitarian state similar to the one imposed in Orwell's classic. Even though Starmer has imposed one of his many U-turns in government and is only proposing the introduction of digital identification on a voluntary basis, it is worth noting that Winston, the main character of 1984, fought to keep freedom of thought, while in 2026, the citizens of Britain are battling to keep freedom of speech. Even though Starmer has climbed down on making Digital identification mandatory, the problem has not been fully resolved, as there is still the possibility of introducing it for all newborn babies.

Another imagination of utopia on earth can be seen in Aldous Huxley's Brave New World, a dystopian world, an imaginary world, a state or society where there is great suffering or injustice. Brave New World believes that monogamous relationships are banned, as well as people having their own thoughts or apparitions. Mood is controlled by drugs, and the state runs people's lives and careers. Everyone is expected to live in a state of utopia and happiness. This opposes God's will for mankind, who he provided free will and the ability to choose their direction and consequently the ability to distinguish right from wrong. In this respect, Lee makes an important point when he recognises that morality is taking a new status independent of the absence of God and in a void which is the cosmos.[116]

Lee sees that intelligence has resulted in the commandments regarding loving God with all your soul and might and being and honouring your father and mother as being optional.[117] Intelligence is eliminating the

---

[115] George Orwell. Page 3-4. In 1984.Wordswoth Classics, Ware, UK. 2021 edition.
[116] Lee, page 36.
[117] Lee, page 38.

idea that good behaviour can culminate in an assertion of goodness. The natural progression and outcome of this thinking is in line with Huxley's principles, which leads to a more indulgent morality that is a breakdown of sexual principles and integrity, and one's inheritances abolished, there will be no need for marriage, or the family unit will disappear. There will be no standards to measure the boundaries of conduct.[118]

A third utopian tale can be seen in Margaret Atwood's The Handmaid's tale where the Gileadean society survives after a nuclear war, with the aristocracy lording over the rest of society. The handmaid's role is to serve their masters and to provide babies for the infertile women of the aristocracy. The only hope is that the drama is set at the end of the 22nd century. The overwhelming outcome of all these utopian novels is that utopia works for the ruling class but is terrifying for everyone else.

---

[118] Lee, page 40-41.

Chapter 3:

The Problem of Labour and The Communist Left

If one meets a powerful person, ask them five questions: 'What power do you have? Where did you get it from? In whose interests do you exercise it? To whom are you accountable? And how do we get rid of you? -Tony Benn[119]

Thomas More once famously stated that "Any person who adopts devious means to win public office should be banned from all of them."

I agree with Billy Bragg's assessment of freedom in the 21st-century context, which is particularly relevant to Britain at the beginning of 2026 and the struggles we face with the current Labour government. Bragg states that the freedom we have has been repackaged as the right to choose, but authentic choice – in housing, at work, and in choosing who to vote for – is difficult to achieve.[120] Therefore, the electorate is fighting to take back control from those who are seeking to take away their liberty, free speech and freedom of choice.[121]

What is in question in Britain today is our ability to convey our thoughts on social media and the freedom to say whatever we think, to whomever we want, whenever we choose, without any form of censorship. However, this opens the door for the need to monitor

---

[119] Quoted from Billy Bragg. The three dimensions of freedom. Faber & Faber, Croydon, UK 2019
[120] Bragg, page 1.
[121] Bragg, page 6.

what is being posted, and in this respect, where do the guidelines need to be drawn? There has to be some accountability; terrorist groups posting what labour states as hate crimes need to be objectively controlled and not selectively controlled. The Labour government are threatening to ban "X," better known as Twitter, from the UK for no reason other than the fact they don't like what is posted on the platform. President Trump sees this as a major control of freedom of speech in the UK and is threatening a wide range of sanctions if labour carry out their threat.

Critics of Labour tend to agree with President Trump and see it as a further incursion into the British public's right to freedom of speech. What is confusing is that both the Labour party, cabinet members and other Labour MPs and Starmer and indeed Ed Davey and Liberal democrat MPs frequently post on X. Therefore, the grounds for banning X in the UK is that the left wing are losing the argument and Reform UK are gaining support through X, in other words X has become a threat to the Labour government already in free fall.

The importance of keeping social media platforms like X is that, as Bragg eloquently states, "liberty is cherished because it empowers us to think, speak and act as we wish, providing the foundation of freedom."[122] Bragg warns that further dimensions are needed to ensure that liberty is protected from the authoritarians. We must also respect those whose views differ from our own, for example, those who disagree with the government are not far right, racists or Nazis. We are just people who dislike and disagree with the far-left communist agenda creed by the Fabian Society and its supporters.

Is Dennis Hannan correct? Are we moving toward economic oblivion? Hannan reports that the budget was all a lie of fictional proportions, a

---

[122] Bragg page 3.

dishonest deception, a forgery of mythical proportions and a fairy story aimed at the gullible. There was no black hole, and Rachel Reeves knew it. She was giving to airy nothing a local habitation and a name. When Rachel Reeves blamed her tax rises on a deteriorating economy, or on 14 years of Tory rule, or on Brexit, she wasn't just engaging in knockabout. She was cynically misleading everyone.[123] Labour have raised taxes as a choice of policy and consequently is punishing those who are employed in order to further compensate those who receive benefits. It is choosing to make employment prohibitive to an extent that ten percent of working-age adults declare that they are too unwell to be considered for employment.[124]

Labour Government Lies

Camilla Tominey has written an excellent article in The Telegraph on December 12th 2025, indicating that Starmer's hypocrisy is mind-bogglingly even by the low standards set by Westminster. In the first place, Starmer insists that Reeves' budget on November 26th 2025, did not break the Labour Party's 2024 manifesto promise not to raise taxes on working people. However, Tominey points out that maintaining the income tax threshold undoubtedly hurts people in employment by taking more money out of their hard-earned pay slips and is considered to be an impotent lie.[125]

Secondly, labour have consistently claimed that there was a £30 billion deficit and that the electorate was misled because in reality there was a £4.2 billion excess. This can be linked to Starmer's claim that the average public house will experience a 4% rise in hospitality business rates, while in reality it increases nearer to 15% in 2026 and will rise by

---

[123] David Hannan. Labour's lies have put Briain on the road to economic oblivion: We are returning for the first-time since Dennis Healey, to high taxation and high spending as a moral choice. Daily Telegraph 28 November 2025.
[124] David Hannan
[125] Camilla Tominey. The twelve lies of Keir Starmer. The Telegraph 12 December 2025

76% over the next three years. Is this policy linked to Labour's close ties with Muslims, who would want to see alcohol consumption prohibited in the UK as it is in all other Muslim countries around the world? This lie has led to over 1,000 pubs banning Labour MPs from their premises.

One pub owner indicated that his costs would increase by £62,000 per year and that pubs were being taxed to oblivion by Starmer. Another lie coming from Starmer is trying to convince us that energy bills have gone down, and he claims that he has cut energy bills by £150 a year for millions of families from April 2026. The reality is that the average energy bill has risen by £187, according to the Centre for Policy Studies.

It is clear that households are paying substantially more for their gas and electricity today than they were before Labour came into power. Starmer also claims that there are more teachers under the Labour government than when the Conservatives left office, but in reality, there are 400 fewer teachers in England in 2025 than when Labour came to power in 2024. However, this is only the tip of the iceberg, as many schools under the budget constraints are not renewing contracts of highly experienced teachers or opting to employ newly qualified or inexperienced teachers in order to keep within budget and keep the costs down.[126]

Starmer promised that police officers would increase by 3,000 additional officers, but official figures show an overall drop of 1,303, a 0.9% drop in officers, as Labour came to power.

The Labour Government, under the auspices of Chancellor Rachel from Accounts, started an attack on the elderly and vulnerable by

---

[126] Tominey

cutting winter fuel payments. Only 1.5 million individuals would receive fuel payments compared to the 10.8 million pensioners prior to the Labour Government.[127]

The announcement was not well received, and concerns included pushing more pensioners into poverty and resulting in more deaths due to the cold winter weather so prevalent in the UK. This was followed by the Education Secretary's announcement that a higher education funding review would take place, which resulted in an increase in tuition fees for the next five years, which was an abandonment of a key Labour principle of the abolition of toxic tuition fees. The annual increases were to be 3.1% for the next five years.

Tax Rises

There are seven ways the cost of living has risen under Labour. The chancellor's two tax-raising budgets have been blamed for increasing inflation, and despite the promise by Labour not to increase income tax on working people, this pledge can be considered to be in tatters, as the personal tax-free allowance of £12,570 is frozen until at least April 2031.

Consequently, millions of workers will end up paying more income tax as more of their annual pay rises will be included in tax funds. In total, the Labour Government has increased taxes by a staggering £67 billion. Connected to increases in the minimum wage, supermarkets have increased food prices.

In conjunction, council tax is increasing each year in most instances by 5%. Gas and electricity bills are also rising, and with Labour's Net Zero levies accounting for 60% of the cost of energy from April 2026, water

---

[127] Cornwall, page 67.

bills have also risen. This is in light of the Water Company's poor control of sewage.

As labourers are finding out at their costs, high taxes can reduce revenue rather than increase it, with many of the richest people leaving the country, and big business moving abroad to avoid paying the high taxes imposed by Rachel Reeves and the Labour Party.[128] This is borne out by the slump in jobs, which is at the fastest rate in five years, with unemployment at 5.1% in January 2026. Younger workers have suffered the most in the weakening job market. People aged 25 to 34 have seen payrolled jobs fall by 167,486 since October 2024, while across all age groups, jobs were down 219,936.[129]

Net Zero

Then the Stupid Debt Zero policy, which aimed to transform the UK into some sort of energy-efficient superpower and aimed to develop hundreds of thousands of new jobs.[130]

The net zero policy, which they claim will provide jobs and reduce energy bills, but unemployment under Labour has risen to its highest level in four years. By the beginning of 2026, it was at 5.1%, and energy bills had risen by over £200 a year for the average family. The slump in jobs is at the fastest rate in 5 years. When we see this and the continuing claims that labour is making life better for the British people, cynicism sets in. When the chancellor tells the country that taxes are rising because of a £22 billion shortfall, while in reality the finances were £4 billion in credit, then it is clear that labour have lied to the country over and over.

---

[128] Truss, page 256.
[129] Chris Price, Eir Nolsea. Jobs slump at fastest rate in five years. The Telegraph. 220 January 2026.
[130] Cornwall, page 69

According to the Institute of Economic Affairs, net zero could cost Britain billions more than officials estimate. Recent analysis supports the finding that the total costs of net zero could exceed the highest official predictions of £7.6 trillion. The official Ed Miliband estimates of the net zero costs are delusional. The Labour Government have persistently undervalued the cost of sustainable energy, heat pumps and electric vehicles, while assuming supposedly low costs of borrowing money to support the fiasco.[131]

Net zero policies are flawed because without the biggest creators of carbon emissions (China, India and the USA, which create approximately 66% of CO_2 emissions) coming on board, then carbon zero will have no impact worldwide. REFORM UK councils save the taxpayer £40 million by scrapping net zero.

The biggest impact on global warming is urbanisation, deforestation versus concrete-rich cities. Deforestation is a triple whammy. **1.** It causes the loss of a crucial ally in reducing excess carbon from the atmosphere. **2.** More emissions occur when felled trees release carbon. **3.** What replaces forests includes: livestock, crops, and houses, all of which contribute to increased carbon emissions by ~25%.[132] Britain should aim to be energy independent by 2040, using oil and gas as well as nuclear and renewables. We are in an excellent position to become a net energy exporter, given the area of sea that surrounds our islands and our expertise in nuclear power. We need to think about abolishing the Climate Change Act and adopting a Climate Freedom Act. Net zero just doesn't work.[133]

---

[131] Net zero could cost Britain billions more than officials estimate, warns new IEA paper — Institute of Economic Affairs 13 January 2026.

[132] Rainforest Alliance. What is the relationship between deforestation and climate change? 12 August 2018.

[133] Truss, page 56.

Local Elections Cancelled and Restored

Noah Eastwood, The Telegraph, January 5th 2026. In an immoral war on democracy, the Labour Government has cancelled local elections, which would deny the right to vote of an estimated 4 million people.

It was believed that 30 councils tried to postpone elections, keeping hundreds of mainly Labour councillors in employment, when in all likelihood they would have been voted out. Keir Starmer is terrified of the consequences of the collapse of support for Labour, with a UK Government approval rating for Labour of just 11% in 3rd to 5th January 2026.

The clause, which enables the government to postpone local elections, was introduced by John Prescott, who introduced it into the Local Government Act in 2000, and it was intended for use in extreme circumstances.[134] However, the current Starmer-led Labour government have weaponised the clause to postpone elections that they fear they will lose. Unless Reform UK wins its judicial review into the postponement of local elections, then postponements could become a rolling programme to suit an unpopular and hated government.

More than 30 councils confirmed that they wanted to delay elections, which were mostly Labour-controlled councils, in an attempt to pervert democracy. This led Reform UK to launch a judicial review to force the government to go ahead with the elections. Reform UK accused Starmer of being frightened of the electorate at a time when the polls show a collapse of support for Labour.[135] There are calls for

---

[134] Gordon Rayner. From Prescott to Rayner, how Labour weaponised obscure clause to dodge democracy. The Telegraph. 14 January 2026.

[135] Daniel Martin, Gordon Rayner, Pieter Snepvangers. Four million denied a vote in attack on democracy. The Telegraph. 14 January 2026.

a change in the law to prevent a "conflict of interest" that enables governments to stop people from having the democratic right to vote. Labour needed to face the electorate and be defeated; it is the party's best hope of turning the decline in Labour government support around.[136] Some Labour MPs were also unhappy that elections are being cancelled, arguing that a Labour government should not be taking the vote away from millions of people, and there is clearly a vested interest considering Labour's poor showing in the opinion polls.[137] One of the consequences of the cancellation of local elections has led to resignations of councillors from some of the councils affected by the cancellation of local elections.[138] A further consideration is the backlash from voters who are being denied their democratic right to vote for change, with some business managers arguing that the cancellation of elections would negatively impact their businesses.[139]

Frank Lawton, in The Telegraph, January 15th 2026, argued that most of the Labour councils that have asked to cancel local elections are facing annihilation by Reform UK, with Labour slipping down to 4th place in some instances.[140] The government's argument is that holding these elections would prove expensive and too complicated, but this argument has been refuted, as elections are the central function of democracy and not an illegitimate expense.[141] However, Frank Lawton argued that the best choice for labour would be to go ahead with the elections, as this would bring Reform UK from opposition into power,

---

[136] Daniel Martin, Gordon Rayner, Pieter Stevangers, 4 million people denied a vote in an attack on democracy, The Telegraph, 14th January 2026
[137] Pieter Snepvangers. Labour MPs attack 'unprecedented' decision to cancel elections. The Telegraph 19 January 2026.
[138] Pieter Snepvangers. Councils face revolt over cancelled elections. The Telegraph. 29 January 2026.
[139] Abigail Buchanan. 'It's undemocratic': Why the Speaker's Chorley constituency is in uproar over cancelled elections. The Telegraph. 21 January 2026.
[140] Frank Lawton. Labour should face the electorate, and lose – it is the party's best hope. The Telegraph 16 January 2026.
[141] Simon Ring. I have resigned as a councillor to fight against Labour's attack on democracy. The Telegraph. 27 January 2026.

and if they do well, then that is good for Britain. However, if they do badly, then this would provide the uni-parties an opportunity to both scrutinise and benefit from their failures. The early resignations mean that there is time to set up by-elections for May 7th 2026, the same day that the original council elections were due to take place.

Lawton used the flagship Kent County Council as a point of question, where Reform UK are in control, and promises big savings. Instead, the £20 million deficit under the Tories has increased to a £60 million deficit under Reform UK. Immigration is the number one factor of discontent. However, it is not as it appears on the surface, as Reform UK are slowly bringing the council budget back under control.

Finally, Lawton gets his wish as expected, then comes the now infamous U-turn from the Starmer government as Starmer abandoned plans to cancel local council elections in May 2026.[142] The decision came just 3 hours after Starmer had promised on National radio that there would be no more U-turns in his government. However, on February 16th 2026 and just two days before a court case brought by Reform UK to challenge the cancellation of elections for 4.6 million people, Starmer capitulated. The reason for the U-turn was that the government were advised by their lawyers that delaying the council elections was illegal. Surely, they should have received that advise before they decided to try to cancel elections? This was a huge win for Reform UK and their determination to challenge the cancellation of elections by being awarded a judicial review.[143] The U-turn by Starmer has surely turned the tide of broken Britain, as the Reform UK tsunami is about to hit British politics. The restoration of the council elections came as a bitter blow to both Labour and the Conservatives as they

---

[142] Ben Riley-Smith, Tom Diver, Fiona Parker. Starmer abandons plan to cancel local elections. The Telegraph, 16 February 2026.
[143] Nigel Farage. Labour is setting a chilling precedent for British democracy. The Telegraph, 14 February 2026.

face wipe out in the councils that attempted to cancel the elections. Interestingly, neither Rupert Lowe and his Restore Britain party nor Ben Hadad and his Advance party challenged the cancellation of elections.

It is clear that Labour is in retreat as they show that there are further damaging revelations as Labour activists are alleged to have spent £36,000 to discredit British journalists who questioned the source of funding for Labour's think tank.[144] The most condemning factor is the deliberate attempt to undermine the free press in a democracy, especially when conducted by a group that holds a large portion of influence over the government. The wheels are beginning to come off a Labour government whose mantra appears to be that the Labour government can do whatever they wish to do under the illusion that they have a mandate from the electorate to enforce laws and decisions on the people that it did not have in its manifesto.

Free Speech

Bragg defines neoliberalism, which is so prevalent in the Western world, as a means of a global market through the development of a single market that does not perceive an individual country's borders, nor the jurisdiction of nations, as it pursues profit.[145] However, the drawback of a global market is the reinforcement of the migration of people, profits and jobs, between countries and even between continents, resulting in the avoidance of government control.

The belief that the free movement of goods and services between countries has lowered prices for consumers. Bragg quotes Adam Smith

---

[144] Tom Harris. The thuggish politics of the Labour Party have been revealed. The Telegraph, 16 February 2026.
[145] Bragg, page 11

as being the advocate that the free market would be regulated by an invisible hand, but is that hand a hand for good, which would benefit all, or a hand for evil, which would benefit the rich and privileged at the expense of everybody else?[146]

Smith believed that competition, rather than freedom from regulation, was the invisible hand that made the free market function. Thomas More said, if I propose sound laws to some ruler and try to eradicate the sources of evil within him, don't you think that I would be summarily thrown out or made an object of ridicule?[147] What if I asserted to the government that all our proposals are both shameful and dangerous to the government, whose honour, even safety, depends on the wealth and support of the British people rather than on their own ideology?[148]

Who is keener to change things than the person who is most dissatisfied with the present manner of life? So, when I reflect on the remarkably wise and holy institutions of the Utopians, who managed with a minimum of laws to run things so well that while virtue is rewarded, yet there is an abundance for all, since everything is divided equally, I contrast their customs with those of so many nations that are forever generating new laws which are not satisfactorily regulated.[149] It's just not possible to live properly where all things are held in common.

How can there be an adequate supply of goods if any individual can withdraw from work, seeing that he is rendered lazy by reliance on the efforts of others?[150] The nature of free speech states that "I disapprove

---

[146] Bragg, page 19
[147] Thomas More. Utopia, page 43. Penguin Classics, London, UK, 2012.
[148] More, page 47
[149] More, page 52
[150] More, page 53

of what you say, but I will defend to the death your right to say it"
(Evelyn Beatrice Hall, quote originally attributed to Voltaire). Free
speech alone is not enough to guarantee freedom. In order to be truly
free, we have to respect everyone's right to express their views.[151] I
believe there is a pivotal link between free speech and equal rights that
are part of the foundations of democracy. I don't intend to bow down
to woke-generated political correctness and am more than happy to
join Eric Weinstein's intellectual dark web and be a pariah to the
Labour, Lib Dems and Greens' communist, anti-democratic agenda. If
free speech is to be maintained, then it must respect the right of
individuals or groups to tell you the things that you don't want to
hear.[152] If you really want change, you have to vote for that change
(Nigel Farage).

Brexit

It is no secret that the Labour Government want closer ties with the
European Union and wants to reverse the referendum result that most
Britons voted for to leave the European Union, and with good cause.
However, not everyone in the Labour government is on board with
closer ties with the European Union. Some Labour MPs are anxious
that closer bonds with Brussels would be a betrayal of Brexit, and
Labour MPs predominantly in constituencies that voted to leave are
worried about the potential impact this may have on their re-
electability.[153] The bottom line is that any Labour MP who thinks that
the UK can re-enter the customs union or the single market without

---

[151] Bragg, page 45
[152] Bragg, page 65
[153] Dan Bloom and Noah Keate. Meet the Labour tribes trying to shape Britain's Brexit reset. Politico. 8
January 2026.

surrendering the freedom we currently have is not living in the real world.[154]

Arguments about whether Brexit was a good thing or a bad thing are irrelevant if we don't answer the question of what we want to do with it afterwards.[155] The logical progress would be to reduce regulatory burdens and red tape, put in place more new trade deals, control immigration and boost our economy. Brexit was botched by the Conservatives, and the hatchet job on Brexit is being carried out by the present Labour government. Brexit gave us the opportunity and freedom to rebuild our economy, control our borders, back British industry, and chart our own pathway in the world.[156] Instead, we have had years of timid leadership, half measures, and a host of politicians who never truly believed in leaving the EU in the first place and as a consequence of the ineptitude of politicians, we find a broken Britain.

However, the good news on Brexit is that Reform UK, when they come into power, will complete the Brexit agreement, as Nigel Farage has always claimed Brexit was botched by the Conservatives and was never done properly (see more in the chapter on What we are aiming for).

Identity Cards

For several decades, especially under Tony Blair's government, identity cards were seriously considered in the UK.[157]

The blunder was that they failed to build support for projects, especially when they gave no indication of the need for the ID cards,

---

[154] Bloom and Keate.
[155] Truss, page 19.
[156] Joseph Boam. X post, 4 February 2026.
[157] Anthony King and Ivor Crewe, page 295. In The bunders of our governments. One World Publications, London, UK, 2014

and it is seen as an infringement of human rights and totalitarian to impose them on the British people, who clearly do not want them. Bragg argues that "the three dimensions of freedom are liberty, equality and accountability, and accountability is the antidote to authoritarianism."[158] Without it, we would never be truly free.

The official slogan of the Leave campaign was, *Let's take back control*, but the Brexit agreement with the EU fell far short of taking back total control. The deciding factor for leaving the EU is that the UK politicians had surrendered the power to veto any laws that were detrimental to the UK, and the power to control the UK came from Brussels, not from Westminster.[159]

In the 1980s, the Tories began to consider introducing ID cards as a programme to strengthen the powers of the police.[160] Another approach was to introduce ID cards to fight against football hooliganism, social security fraud, fights against drug use, truancy, underage drinking, illegal immigration and terrorism.

The Home Office Committee suggested that voluntary ID cards could be introduced in 1990. Those in favour of introducing ID cards tried to market them as something similar to a broad-spectrum antibiotic.[161] They argued that they were generally accepted in most European countries and that they would be of great benefit, especially in identifying criminals, eliminating innocent people from police investigations and tracking illegal immigrants. Indeed, ID cards were rolled out by the Blair government in 2008 for foreign nationals living in the UK. In 2009-2010, ID cards were made available in north-

---

[158] Bragg, page 84
[159] Bragg, page 84
[160] King & Crewe, page 297.
[161] King & Crewe, page 299.

western England. However, the scheme was dropped due to the rising costs.

It was proposed that each individual might have to pay up to £93 for the privilege of having an ID card. The scheme to introduce compulsory ID cards was considered flawed and was ultimately defeated in the House of Commons in July 2009. The whole scheme was estimated to have cost £300 million and was a complete waste of money and space.[162]

Those for and against admitted that both introducing and maintaining ID cards would be expensive and hugely complex. ID cards would be easy to forge and to intercept, and digital ID cards could be easily lost or hacked if mobile phones were stolen or cloned. It's worth noting that over 70,000 mobile phones were stolen in London in 2023, with the iPhone 15 Pro Max being the UK's most stolen device, and thefts had increased by 425% since 2021.

The UK accounts for a staggering 39% of all mobile thefts across Europe.[163] As early as the mid-90s, the pressure group Liberty warned ID cards posed a danger because they were a mechanism of government control and would be harmful to citizens' freedom.[164] An estimated 78,000 people in England and Wales had their phones or bags snatched from them on the street in the year ending March 2024, according to the Crime Survey for England and Wales. That figure translates to more than 200 snatch thefts occurring every single day. This marks a 153% increase in such incidents compared to the year ending in March 2023.[165] The theft of mobile phones offers a huge opportunity for organised crime to steal identities, especially if they

---

162 King & Crewe, page 315.
163 Vinnie Mattel, International Business Times, 12th August 2025.
164 King & Crewe, page 302.
165 Patel

were linked to digital ID cards, which would, if fully rolled out, have bank details, passport data, health data and a plethora of other personal information stored on them.

Housing and Benefits

Housing is high on Labour's agenda of manifesto deliverables, and labour aim to build 1.5 million new homes over the next five years. Within this time frame, Labour aims to provide the biggest increase to affordable, council and social housing for a generation. Labour plans to deliver these houses through the Affordable Homes Programme, for which they have allocated £11.5 billion. Labour claims this policy will deliver tens of thousands of new affordable homes by 2026. In the October 2024 budget, Labour have allocated an additional £500m to build another 5,000 homes.[166] However, the completion of houses in England dropped to 190,000 in the 12 months to June 2025, a nine-year low despite the Labour Party's promises to make housing a priority.[167] Labour is planning to house illegal immigrants in new-build social housing. This pledge has been blasted by the media as an outrage, because it prioritises the housing of illegal immigrants ahead of the homeless, British people already on the housing list and veterans.[168] The £100 million scheme, which empowers councils to build new properties solely for immigrants, has accumulated approximately 200 enquiries from local authorities. Councils will be able to use the funding to either build new properties or refurbish existing ones.

---

[166] Scott Cabot. From policy to reality: Delivering Labour's affordable housing targets. CBRE 16 January 2025.
https:// www.cbre.co.uk/insights/articles/from-policy-to-reality-delivering-labours-affordable-housing-targets
[167] Adam McCowan. Is Britains economy broken? Page 51. Self-publication 2025
[168] Aaron Newbury. Labour blasted over plan to house migrants in new-build social homes – 'utter disgrace!' Express online 31 December 2025

The number of people receiving benefits from Britain without having to work has massively increased by 1.5 million since Labour took office, with new figures revealing that nearly 4.2 million people on Universal Credit now have "no work requirements" following a surge in mental health claims.[169]

The government is facing increasing pressure over soaring welfare funding amid the backlash against Chancellor Rachel Reeves's tax-raising "Benefits Street" Budget. According to official data, in December, there were 4.2 million people on Universal Credit with no requirement to work, up from the 2.7 million inherited by Labour in July 2024. These individuals make up half of the 8.4 million who are on the benefit overall, marking the largest increase in claimants since the start of the COVID pandemic.[170] Opponents claim the numbers demonstrate that Labour had lost control after it was forced to U-turn on intended cuts to sickness benefits in 2025. Lee Anderson, the Reform UK MP, said: "This is further evidence that Labour favours the shirkers in this country, not the workers. The welfare system is abused by people who don't need it and people who aren't even citizens of this country. "Only Reform has a clear plan to overhaul our benefits system, cut the ballooning £342 billion welfare bill and get people back into work."[171]

---

[169]Nick Gutteridge, Ollie Corfe. Labour hands 'no need to work' benefits to 1.5m more people. The Telegraph 20 January 2026.
[170]Michael D. Carroll. Labour's 'no work requirements' benefit bombshell sees 1.5M added under Starmer's watch Express online 21 January 2026.
[171]Nick Gutteridge, Ollie Corfe. Labour hands 'no need to work' benefits to 1.5m more people. The Telegraph 20 January 2026.

Housing Market and The Pending Fiscal Disaster

The lack of affordable housing in the UK has become a huge economic barrier to Britain's growth and vitality.[172] A lot of houses have been bought by international corporations, and in many parts of the country, it is prohibitive in reality to lease a property. This has a knock-on effect of stopping people from moving from location to location in Britain to search for jobs. High taxes on landlords do not seem to have any impact on freeing up houses in the rental market. Furthermore, there is the risk that Labour's property market drive to build 300,000 homes a year could seriously damage the value of houses for home owners who have paid off their mortgages and are dependent on the value of their homes to help fund their retirement.[173] There is a clear shortage of houses, and there appears to be a balancing act between maintaining the value of houses for homeowners while building sufficient affordable houses so that young people can get on the property ladder. However, there is the additional factor that the Labour government has to find housing for the massive influx of immigrants, legal and illegal, which could further force young British people out of the housing market. This comes in light of the fact that Labour has pledged to improve living standards for people in the UK, while the reality is that there is clear evidence that the standard of living is declining under Starmer's government.[174] The Office for National Statistics reports that GDP per capita has shrunken in the final six months of 2025 due to rising taxes, price rises and lower than expected pay rises. This leads to a reduction in disposable income, and therefore, they have less

---

[172] Ross Clark, page 265.

[173] Pui-Guan Man. Labour's property market plot could hammer your house price. The Telegraph, 14 February 2026.

[174] Emma Taggart. Labour's pledge to boost living standards lies in tatters. The Telegraph, 12 February 2026.

money available to save up for a deposit to get on the property ladder and their hopes of owning their own homes have disappeared. The prediction is that people's disposable income will grow less under the current Labour government than at any other time since records began.[175]

It has become a vicious cycle that seems at this moment in time unbreakable unless there is a huge step down by the chancellor and the treasury to reverse the trend. Furthermore, there is a growing belief that Rachel from accounts is "boiling the economy alive," and there will be insufficient tax revenue to cover the chancellor's spending intentions.[176] Piece by piece, the strain of high taxes, increased spending, and irrational spending is demolishing the economy's ability to increase sufficiently to escape fiscal calamity and failure.[177]

Assisting in The Prosecution of British Troops

The more news that emerges regarding Starmer and the current Labour government, the more evil and hypocrisy emerge. The hypocrisy of Starmer can be seen in the fact that he allegedly stood up for British troops when they were castigated by Donald Trump as not contributing very much in the Afghanistan conflict, but was associated with the human rights law on legal cases that resulted in the prosecution of British troops who fought in the Iraq conflict.[178] For example, the prosecution of Sergeant Richie Catterall, who fought for Britain in Iraq and Afghanistan and was pursued after he shot dead an Iraqi teacher who was armed with an assault rifle. The hypocrisy of Starmer is that he willingly gave his time free of charge to help investigate British veterans, which is deeply worrying, and the question

---

[175] Emma Taggart.

[176] Andrew Lilico. Reeves is slowly boiling the economy alive. The Telegraph, 12 February 2026.

[177] Andrew Lilico.

[178] Robert Mendick, Tony Diver. Starmer: Use the ECHR to investigate British troops. The Telegraph 28 January 2026.

of who Starmer supports, Britain or those who collaborate to bring the country down, is becoming clearer. Starmer supports himself at the expense of what is right or wrong. Starmer's association with the solicitor Phil Shiner, who was struck off for fraud, brings into question Starmer's moral ability to commit British troops into future conflicts because they run the risk of being prosecuted by the very government that sent them into battle. Reform UK have declared that it will leave the ECHR if they win the next election. The clear advantage of leaving the ECHR is that it would enable Britain to recover control over human rights law in Britain and not be at the mercy of Strasbourg. Several cases have included killers, rapists and illegal immigrants who were set to be deported back to their countries of origin, escaping deportation due to Article 8 of the ECHR, which values family life above misdemeanours.[179]

Controversies: Chagos Islands and The Mandelson Affair

Starmer has been a one-man crusade in attempting to give the Chagos Islands away to Mauritius, a close ally of China.[180] In trying to give away the Chagos Islands to Mauritius at an estimated cost of £35 billion to the UK taxpayer, it shows how treacherous and unpatriotic Starmer actually is. The agreement involves the UK conceding sovereignty of the Chagos Islands to Mauritius and then renting back the Diego Garcia military base.[181] Mr Trump had previously condemned the agreement as an "act of great stupidity" and an "act of total weakness." Mr Trump alleged the island, including the site of the vital military

---

179 Robert Mendick, Tony Diver
180 Daniel Hannan. Starmer's Chagos fanatics are determined to ensure the surrender goes ahead. The Telegraph. 24 January 2026.
181 Sophie Wingate, David Hughes.US and UK agree to work closely on Chagos Islands military base. The Independent 3 February 2026.

base, was being forfeited "for no reason whatsoever."[182] Yet, despite some opposition from within Labour ranks and opposition from the House of Lords, Starmer continues to attempt to give away the Chagos Islands in a sheer act of madness.

Another major controversy facing Starmer is the appointment of Peter Mandelson as ambassador to the USA. It is a nightmare for Starmer that just won't go away, and the more Starmer tries to hide it, the more revelations of Mandelson's relationship with the paedophile Jeffrey Epstein threaten to bury the already besieged Prime Minister. The BBC declaring that the Mandelson revelations are a scandal on another level aptly summarises the depth of the problem for Starmer.[183] This coincides with the fact that Mandelson is now being investigated over allegations that he leaked government information to Epstein when he was business secretary in Gordon Brown's government.[184] The question arises as to why Starmer appointed Mandelson as an ambassador to the USA when his relationship with Epstein was already known?[185] Mandelson leaked confidential government papers to Epstein, and the extent of those leaks is the focus of a police investigation. What was most demining is that Starmer was forced to disclose that he knew about Mandelson's ongoing friendship with Epstein, even after Epstein was a convicted paedophile. It is this disclosure that resulted in Starmer being disowned by his own MPs and increased the hatred of the people against him.[186] The outcome of the police investigation and its impact on Starmer will be of interest to everyone.

---

182 Wingate and Hughes

183 Chris Mason. Mandelson revelations a scandal on another level. BBC News 4 February 2026.

184 Joshua Nevett. Police investigate Mandelson over claims he leaked information to Epstein. BBC News. 3 February 2026.

185 Nevett.

186 Gordon Rayner. Disowned by his MPs, despised by the public, Starmer must know the game is up. The Telegraph 4 February 2026.

Rape Gangs

The grooming gangs scandal hits new depths of deprivation with the revelation that Starmer has ordered the destruction of millions of court case records to cover up his government's role in the crimes.[187] The question arises, "Is it legal?" Does the government have the power to order the deletion of magistrates' court records? The court records that are about to be destroyed could reveal the true extent of the rape gangs and that they were far more extensive than previously envisaged. This could result in further embarrassment to the already beleaguered government, and thus, they are attempting to destroy the evidence before it comes into the public domain.

Labour Government Approval Ratings

What should we expect going forward? Just when you thought it couldn't get any worse for the Labour government, their approval ratings sink to even greater depths.[188] The net rating now stands at -59, with 70% disapproving of the government and just 11% approving, with 19% saying they don't know. New polls show that Labour has lost nearly 50% of its supporters from the 2024 general election. Even more concerning, it is losing backing to both parties on the Left and Right, with 11% of 2024 Labour voters saying they will vote for Reform UK and 8% saying they now support the Liberal Democrats. Labour has already lost 8% of its supporters to the Green Party, and this figure is estimated to rise even higher as more Labour supporters become disillusioned with Starmer and his government.

---

[187] Katie Lam. Is Labour trying to cover up fresh revelations about the grooming gang scandal? The Telegraph, 15 February 2026.
[188] Andrew Papworth. Labour crashes to devastating new low as bombshell poll shows record unpopularity. 10 January 2026 Express on line

Labour and The Fear of Tyranny

Democracy fails because the electorate converts to an augmented totalitarian regime. The Fabian Society's approach to socialism by evolution, not revolution, sums up the approach to a more totalitarian society perfectly. Democracy fails by being attacked from within, and they are not normally overcome by outside powers, such as an incursion or violent uprising.[189] According to Sherelle Jacobs, tyranny comes to Britain by cancelling elections, and authoritarian governments test out what they can manipulate unchallenged.[190]

Where elections end, tyranny begins.[191] Paper ballots are needed because they cannot be tampered with and can be recounted. Life is political, not because the world cares about us, but because the world reacts to what we do.[192] In the politics of everyday living, our words and our gestures count a lot and have an impact on others.

Unless you understand what is wrong, you cannot correct it, and if you remain silent, there will come a time when tyranny will take over, and it will be too late to let your voice be known in the public arena. To paraphrase Sir Winston Churchill, "History will be nice to Reform UK because we will write it ourselves." If we are to be successful, we need to both engage with the internet and utilise but at the same time separate ourselves from the constraints and propaganda on the internet. We need to be true to our calling and not be deceived by the dark side of Advance or claims to restore Britain that have no foundations in reality.

---

[189] Jonathan Sumption. Page 3, in The Challenge of democracy: And the rule of law, Profile Books, London, UK, 2025.
[190] Sherelle Jacobs. This is how tyranny comes to Britain. The Telegraph, 15 January 2026.
[191] Timothy Snyder. Page 30 in On Tyranny: Twenty lessons from the twentieth century. The Bodley Head Publishers, London, UK, 2017.
[192] Snyder, page 33.

If you want to understand what is happening in Britain, you have to understand the four means by which the truth is discarded on the way to a totalitarian state. The first tactic is a hostility toward confirmable reality and truth by continually presenting a lie as the truth.[193] For example, Starmer's claim that he values free speech when the evidence shows that he is doing everything in his power to limit or prohibit free speech. A second example is by labelling all those who oppose his lies as far-right racists and unpatriotic. The second means to undermine democracy is by spiritualistic and extramundane repetition of the phrases in the hope that the public will believe the lies,[194] for example, that all "Reform UK members are far-right racists." The continued repetition of Nigel Farage and Reform UK at the Labour party conference in Liverpool in 2025 is a classic example, which led one cartoonist to state that he was going to attend the Reform UK conference in 2026 because they don't talk about Farage all the time. The third approach to a totalitarian state is the complete adoption and support of contradiction.[195] For example, the Labour government's promise to lower energy bills by £250 per household, while the reality is that energy bills have risen due to the government's policy. Or the claim that labour has improved the cost of living for all working-class families in Britain, when the statistics clearly show that the cost of living has declined for most people in Britain under the Labour government. Accepting these lies requires the desertion of the truth and rationality.[196] The final means by which a totalitarian state comes into existence is through the misplaced faith in a government that is clearly failing and trusting the government when they claim that they are acting in the best interests of the country.[197] The truth can be

---

[193] Snyder, page 66.
[194] Snyder, page 66-67.
[195] Snyder, page 67.
[196] Snyder, page 68.
[197] Snyder, page 68.

measured through YouGov polls that show that Starmer's popularity among UK voters continues to fall, with 18 percent supporting him and 63 percent disliking him.[198]

As Snyder points out, beware when governments try to limit freedom in the name of safety, such as the need to introduce identity cards in order to keep us safe.[199] To be patriotic is to do everything one can to promote the country and serve in the best interests of the country. This is the foundation and philosophy of Reform UK and opposes the Fabian Society beliefs of the Labour Party. As Snyder has warned us, if we are not prepared to stand against tyranny, then we will perish under it. Britain is broken, and only Reform UK want to fix it.

---

[198] The most popular Labour politicians in the UK | Politics | YouGov Ratings
[199] Snyder, page 101.

Chapter 4:

Fake News, Lies and Accusations

The Role of News in Reporting the Truth

When we consider the role of the media, whether it be online social media or the more traditional newspapers, we can begin to grasp the vast influence the press has over the thought processes of individuals. For example, Theresa May was undone, inevitably by the impossibility of delivering Brexit that was both desirable and feasible and by Boris Johnson's betrayal behind her back.[200] Yet much of the rhetoric was played out in the media.

O'Brien highlighted some viewers' views on the BBC long before the Trump and Gaza biased reporting, and some of the comments about the BBC included in his book included "why is the BBC allowed to get away with being so biased? It is said to be riddled with communists." "I now find the BBC is a platform for every self-acknowledged enemy of Britain. "The immense propaganda machine of the BBC and the press is against the people."[201] Personally, I'm one of those people who have stopped watching the BBC news channels and radio programmes because they just make me angry. I would welcome the TV license being scrapped, and I have joined GB News because Nigel Farage and Jacob Rees-Mogg have programmes on that channel which I can sit

---

[200] James O'Brien. How they broke Britain, page 82.
[201] O'Brien page 86.

through and listen to their arguments and those of their guests without getting angry.

Soppel says that Nigel Farage's politics are to the right, but he's always been a hack first; he's always primarily a political activist, an agitator. The description of Farage as right of centre doesn't quite cut it. He is way too the right of centre. Reports of the imminent death of GB News turned out to be greatly exaggerated. A very different television news piece was emerging, and it was gaining traction and audience. Advertisers were taking a second look. It was clear its influence was growing on the right of British politics, and all sorts of darlings of the conservative right were finding a lucrative way to supplement their meagre parliamentary earnings. Lee Anderson, Jacob Rees-Mogg, Esther McVeigh, who was appointed under Sunak as the Minister for Common Sense, and her husband and fellow MP Philip Davis were all given births on the channel. No Labour or Liberal Democrat MP was offered the same. Money isn't everything, but a survey by The Guardian, based on the declaration in the MP's Register of Interest, found that while GB News had paid just £1,000 in contribution fees to Labour parliamentarians, it had paid a whopping £660,000 to the Tories.[202]

Jacob Reece Mogg, the former Business Secretary and Leader of the House, delivering breaking news as though he were some kind of latter-day Walter Cronkite. And though Ofcom has repeatedly ruled against GB News, it has all the effectiveness of a teacher who has lost control of the class. The blurring of news and comment was becoming ever murkier. Ofcom has ruled that shows hosted by Reece Mogg, Esther McVeigh and Philip Davies broke rules which state that politicians should not usually front news coverage and warned that the

---

[202] Jon Sopel, page 203-204. In Strangeland: Is this Britain's new normal. Penguin Random House, London, UK, 2025.

channel was on notice about future breaches. The Ofcom Code states that a politician shouldn't be a newsreader, reporter or interview others in a news programme unless, exceptionally, it is editorially justified. They can, however, front non-news programmes. This can be argued that it is acceptable for politicians to head non-news generated programmes, but the objection would be that the channel is called GB News and therefore all programmes generate the news[203] When GB News was launched, the aim might have been to be right of centre, but as time has passed there has been political drift in an unmistakable direction which makes the question of Foxification of British News a real probability, particularly given the apparent reluctance of the regulator to step in and prevent this trend. Like the partakers that now muscle and shriek all other birds out of the way in our London parks and gardens, a non-native invasive species is threatening to take over our long-standing way of doing broadcast news.[204]

Moving on to other news channels, scrutiny has been focused on the BBC. As Jon Sopel has eloquently described, in news covering news in Jordan, an edict comes down on high from the BBC, where the BBC boss says we mustn't say this or that.[205] Occasionally, it does. After the Hamas attack in Israel on October 6th 2023, using the word terrorism to describe what they did was ruled out, which is a deformation of the English language.[206] As Sopel points out, if something causes terror, then victims have been terrorised. What other words should you use to describe those who perpetrated the act?[207] It is understandable that the BBC needs to be cautious. In the same context, the current Labour government and the police appear terrified of upsetting Muslims by declaring anything a terrorist attack when carried out by one religious

---

[203] Sopel, page 205
[204]Sopel, page 206
[205]Sopel, page 189
[206] "Terrorist" - Why the BBC doesn't use the word. 5 minutes on. 11 October 2023
https://www.bbc.co.uk/programmes/p0gkwwtb
[207]Sopel, page 189

group against another. It is a good thing to be cautious when you are concerned to report the news accurately and not mislead the public, but it is not acceptable when the motive is to hide the truth or worse, deliberately mislead the public. Live reporting demands that you tread carefully on what you say on air because once said, it cannot be retracted. The last thing you want is a reporter freewheeling, but when that caution becomes self-censorship, that's damaging.[208]

Another example of the BBC being cautious was the reporting of Brexit.[209] How many BBC reports and documentaries have there been on the difference it has made to the UK economy? Furthermore, following Brexit, the huge queues at the start of the school summer holidays for people trying to cross the channel, a reporter mentioned that this was the consequence of all passports having to be scrutinised, but never made the connection to Brexit.[210] Also, it was not reported that the British government failed to follow guidance relating to opening more gates where passports could be checked. It was not the reporter's fault as newsroom personnel are sorely aware that Brexit is factious and results in criticism of the BBC.[211]

Breached Guidelines and Fake News

BBC Coverage of the Israel-Hamas War

There is no doubt that the media have an enormous influence over consumers' views and stances, even to the point of affecting their attitudes and emotions on a variety of subjects. Areas that the media affects include politics and how the public perceives certain scenarios, such as political parties, countries at war or during the changing of

---

[208]Sopel, page 189
[209]Sopel, page 189
[210]Sopel, page 189
[211]Sopel, page 189

leaders. For all my adult life, I have relied upon the accuracy of the BBC to keep me informed regarding what is happening in the world. I suspect, like most people, I have never questioned the accuracy, the honesty or integrity of what is being presented in their many news bulletins. That is, until now, with the first indication in 2024 that the BBC may have breached guidelines over the Israel-Hamas war.[212] An internal BBC report into the BBC coverage of the Israel-Hamas war revealed an extremely alarming practice of bias against Israel. The bias was evident across the BBC's television news, radio broadcasts, online news, podcasts and social media outputs.[213] Particularly, worrying is that the BBC accused Israel of genocide 14 times more than they did with the terrorist Hamas organisation. The report identified 1553 breaches of the BBC's own editorial guidelines, including the impartiality, accuracy, editorial value and public interest guidelines. The BBC consistently minimised the terrorism perpetrated by Hamas, and some BBC reporters showed excessive empathy towards Hamas.

BBC Coverage of President Trump

It is well documented that the BBC doctored its video coverage of President Trump's speech at the White House on January 6th 2021, in its Panorama programme.[214] The BBC spliced two separate parts together to infer that President Trump was inciting the riot on Capitol Hill, which was untrue and deliberately misleading. The Panorama programme also showed the crowd walking towards Capitol Hill as a consequence of President Trump's speech, while in reality the procession had occurred prior to the speech. It is clear that the BBC set out to spread malevolent and vicious lies portraying Trump as a

---

[212] Camilla Turner. BBC 'breached guidelines 1,500 times' over Israel-Hamas war The Telegraph 7 September 2024

[213] Turner.

[214] Victor Nava. BBC 'materially misled viewers' by deceptively editing Trump Jan 6 speech for documentary: Whistleblower. New York Post 3 November 2025.

fascist, right-wing demon.[215] It is clear that the doctoring of video clips has damaged the BBC's reputation and has led to mistrust of its news programmes.[216] The knock-on effect has led the US president to seek $10 billion in damages for defamation and violation of trade practices over the broadcaster's editing of a speech he made in 2021.[217] The BBC, while apologising to the US President, is opposing the lawsuit. Consequently, this has led to the BBC being replaced by GB News as the most trusted and watched news channel by the British people.

In light of the breaches, how do the public view the BBC? In a YouGov poll, 31 percent of people believe the BBC is bias in favour of left-wing views, compared with 19 percent of people who believe the BBC to be bias in favour of right-wing views.[218] Interestingly, 73 percent of Reform UK voters and 52 percent of Conservative voters believe the BBC is left-wing in its reporting, compared with 31 percent of Labour voters who believe the BBC to be right-wing in its news coverage.

If the BBC is bias toward President Trump and toward Israel, how far does the BBC bias extend? It is clear that their coverage of Reform UK and their constant label of Reform being far right and racist comes into the category of misrepresentation of Reform UK and its values. This is clearly seen in the BBC Question Time programme in December 2025, where the BBC deliberately brought illegal migrants into the audience to attack Reform UK and Zia Yusuf's stance on deporting all illegal immigrants. The attack was orchestrated by Fiona Bruce, asking if migrants such as Ashraf (who came here illegally) would be deported

---

[215] Brendan O'Neill. All of Britain – and it's just not one bit is bias. New York Post 10 November 2025.

[216] Stephen castle. What to know about the turmoil at the BBC. New York Times 10 November 2025.

[217] Sky News. Trump v the BBC: What's in the lawsuit and how has the broadcaster responded? 13 January 2026.

[218] Matthew Smith. Is the BBC biased? What the public think following the Davie and Turness resignations. YouGov 10 November 2025.

under a Reform Government?"[219] Zia correctly pointed out that there are legal routes into Britain and that when refugees are fleeing a country, it is the women and children who come first and not 18 to 30-year-old men of fighting age.[220]

BBC License Fee

A record number of Britons refused to pay for their TV licence as another 300,000 households did not renew their licence in the year from March 2024 to March 2025, according to the latest annual report from the BBC. The total number of people paying for a TV licence fee dropped from 24.1 million to 23.8 million in 2025. This equates to 12.5 percent of households that should be paying for a license not paying. The BBC loses almost half a billion pounds in annual revenue because of the rise in the percentage of people evading paying for their TV license.[221]

---

[219] Michael Knowles. Zia Yusuf clashes with small boat migrants during extraordinary Question Time row. Express 4 December 2025.
[220] Knowles.
[221] Taylor Bushey. TV licence fee evasion hits record high as BBC reveals 1 in 8 households dodge fares for rival streamers. GB News 23 July 2025.

Chapter 5:

The rise of Reform UK

It is pertinent to note that at the general election in July 2024, Reform UK had approximately 65,000 members but by the annual conference in Birmingham under the banner of The Next Step membership had risen to approximately 243,000 and on January 19, 2026, the membership stands at 271,520 with over 100,000 new members in 2025 making Reform UK the largest political party in the UK.

It is interesting to note that in the 2024 election, in 137 seats that the Conservatives lost to Labour, a combined Reform and Tory vote would have secured the seat. After the general election, the mood was sombre, one of relief, following the general election. The change to Labour was due to exhaustion with the Tories, not due to a passion for Labour. Therefore, telling the truth about things is simply finding out what the facts are and then complying with the factual statements in order to lead people in the correct direction. By August 2024, the splits began to be revealed in Labour's meticulously prepared guise.[222]

Nigel Farage is thought to be in touch with the British people and way ahead of the metropolitan elite in recognising the defining challenges of our time. This Trust believes that Nigel Farage has been prophetic on the dangers of uncontrolled migration, the dangers of the ECHR, the impact of Net Zero and the dangers of radical Islam.[223] Reform UK stands for common sense politics, and it stands for British culture, identity and values.[224] People are fed up with being treated as second-

---

[222] Cornwall, page 66.
[223] Truss, page 334.
[224] William Lepone. Reform UK. What Britains fastest rising party stands for. LocalGov, 29 May 2025.

class citizens in their own country. Reform UK values are ones that the majority of British people can identify with. It is easy to feel at home with the Reform UK party.

Reform Election Candidates

It was good to note that Reform UK is not a rescue charity for every scared Conservative MP who wants to save their livelihood and remain as an MP in the face of Conservative annihilation at the next general election.[225] Any existing MPs who want to join Reform must be committed to Reform's pledges and manifesto promises, and Reform will be selective on whether it will allow MPs from other parties to join Reform. Indeed, Zia Yusef has indicated that he has received many messages from Reform grassroots members worried about existing MPs from other political parties joining Reform.[226] Zia made it clear that Reform grassroots members will be prioritised during candidate selection for the next class of MPs and not failed former Tory MPs. The refreshing part of Zia's communication was his acknowledgement that grassroot members built the party into what it is today. Undoubtedly, among the current Reform UK councillors and 272,708 members, there will be many with ambitions to become Reform UK MPs. In light of all the hard work done by the Wokingham branch where I live, I would personally like to see one of my colleagues chosen as the candidate for the next general election rather than a failed Tory wanting to get back into parliament.

Grassroot members have largely been successful in helping Reform UK to win 10 councils in the May 2025 local elections, and the continued success of Reform UK in a number of by-elections since May 2025. By the beginning of February 2026, Reform UK had won

---

[225] Nigel Farage. Reform is not a rescue charity for every panicky Tory MP. The Telegraph 17 January 2026.
[226] Zia Yusef. Email to Reform members 3 December 2025.

72 by-election seats and made further inroads in demolishing the so-called Labour red wall. A more notable by-election win was the win in Ynys Gybi in Wales, beating Plaid Cymru. There are likely to be more notable by-election wins as by-elections are taking place on a weekly basis, leading into the 7 May 2026 local elections.

Reform UK has to continue its momentum and build on the successes of 2025 by achieving further successes in the local elections that are to take place across the UK on 7 May 2026. As Nigel has stated, these will be the biggest political battles in Britain before the next general election. There has been some encouraging news with local election success at the beginning of 2026, but also a warning that there is still a lot of hard work to be done. Councillors across the country can see what is happening. They know their old parties no longer listen, no longer represent ordinary people, and no longer stand for anything meaningful. Reform UK is the only place for those who want actual transformation from the decline we are witnessing.[227]

One warning sign early in 2026 is the loss of the council seat in Horsley, Derbyshire, to the Green Party. This was offset by a win in Flintshire and the continued inroads into Scotland and the win from Labour in Codnor, Langley Milland Aldercar with a 45.6% gain of the vote, however Advance put out their first ever candidate in this seat and gained 12.3% of the vote and they may be a dangerous opponent at the next general election as they may split the Reform vote and allow Labour back into power.

---

[227] David Bull. Weekly newsletter. 18 January 2026

Defections and Supporters

There has almost been a floodgate of defections from the Conservative party to Reform UK over the past 18 months, and it is unlikely to have stopped with Nigel Farage keeping the door ajar, if not fully open, until 7 May 2026, the day of this year's local council elections. It is important to understand why so many Conservatives are defecting to Reform UK, given the illusion that Reform UK are a far-right fascist organisation, which is utter nonsense. Lee Anderson became Reform UK's first MP because he wanted his country back and was voted in as a Reform MP in the 2024 general election.[228] Lucy Allen was next to follow in May 2024, in the lead up to the general election, she believed that the Reform party represents traditional centre-right values and priorities, policies and beliefs that the Conservative party have abandoned.[229] Dame Andrea Jenkins defected after originally stating she wouldn't join Reform UK. Her reason for the defection was that she was now "politically aligned" with Reform UK policies, and subsequent to joining Reform, was elected as Mayor of Lincolnshire in May 2025. Aidan Burley, a former MP for Cannock Chase, joined Reform UK in December 2024, which resulted in Nigel Farage claiming it was "death by a thousand defections" for the Conservatives.[230] Reform UK are well short of a thousand defections, but I like the sentiment. The former Conservative MP Marco Longhi defected to Reform UK in January 2025, stating that the party of Churchill and Thatcher was now unrecognisable.

---

[228] Alix Culbertson. Who are all the former conservative MPs who have defected to Reform? Sky news. 15 January 2026.

[229] Tara Cobham. Tory MP claims she defected to Reform before Conservative Party suspended her. The Independent. 27 May 2024.

[230] Alix Culbertson.

Alan Amos was next to join Reform from the Tories, followed by Ross Thompson, who suggested that only Reform UK possessed the answers to the dilemmas and challenges facing Scotland. Anne Marie Morris joined Reform UK in July 2025 and heads up Reform's social care policy unit. She joined because she believes that Reform "offers the vision and leadership Britain so badly needs."[231] Anne Marie also stated that "The country is in a desperate position. I believe now it is Reform UK that offers the vision and leadership Britain so badly needs. I want to play my part in delivering that vision."[232] David Jones joined the Reform Party as a private individual because the Reform Party best depicts his views. Sir Jake Berry joined Reform because Britain is broken and the Conservatives have lost their way. Adam Holloway joined because Reform UK is the only party that grasps the extent of Britain's danger.[233] With each defection, the message from the defectors gets stronger. Nadine Dorries, who defected the day before the Reform UK conference 2025, aptly entitled "The Next Step," declared that "The Tory party is dead."[234] Danny Kruger, the first shadow cabinet minister to defect from the Conservatives, stated that the Conservative party were over and that there were "toxic elements" within the Conservative Party.[235] Kruger also regrettably admitted that the Conservative government offered 14 years of abject failure. Maria Caulfield, a former health minister, joined a day after Danny Kruger with the sentiment that if your beliefs are right-minded, then Reform UK was the only option, and with the caveat that the people who believed that Brexit would not take place think that Reform will not win the next election are in for a shock. Perhaps more

---

[231] Alix Culbertson.

[232] David Williamson. Ex Tory MP suspended for using the N-word defects to join Reform UK. Express, 2 July 2025.

[233] Alix Culbertson.

[234] Daniel Martin, Ben Riley Smith. Nadine Dorries defects to Reform on eve of party conference. The Telegraph 4 September 2025.

[235] Jennifer McKiernan. Tory MP and shadow minister Danny Kruger defects to Reform. BBC News. 15 September 2025

damning for the Conservatives was the defection of 20 Tory councillors during the 2025 Conservative Party conference.[236]

With each defection, the momentum for Reform increased and accelerated, with to date Reform UK topping every poll since May 2025 and its lead over other political parties grows and grows and is consistently 10 points ahead of its competitors. The next defection was Sarah Atherton, a former defence minister, stating that the Tory party no longer aligned with her values and Britain's armed forces deserved better, an observation that Starmer and his cronies should take on board.[237] Jonathan Gullis joined Reform because the Tories had lost touch with ordinary people. Lia Nici came across from the Tories because she believed she was more Reform in her outlook than most Reform members. Chris Green and Ben Bradley came because the Conservatives and Labour had lost the trust of the British people. As we moved into 2026, the Tories may have been reeling from the extent of defections to Reform UK, but the atomic bomb of defections was about to explode upon a declining dinosaur. Nadhim Zahawi, a former chancellor and vaccines minister during the COVID pandemic, defected to Reform on 12 January 2026, claiming that the Tories were defunct.[238] Mr Zahawi declared that "Britain needs Reform," the reaction from several Tories was one of shock and surprise, with Sir Brandon Lewis stating that Mr Zahawi would be an exceptional asset for Reform.[239] If the defection of Nadhim Zahawi to Reform was akin to an atomic explosion, the defection of Robert Jenrick set off a tsunami in the Tory inner circle. Jenrick came with the headline that the Conservatives "Broke Britain," and claimed that the Tories were

---

[236] Sky News. Twenty Tory councillors' defect to Reform - as Badenoch insists party having 'good conference. 7 October 2025
[237] Alix Culbertson.
[238] Alix Culbertson.
[239] Domonic Penna. Zahawi accused of tantrum politics after defecting to Reform UK. The Telegraph. 13 January 2026.

no longer fit for purpose, they were dishonest and rotten, fighting talk from the former shadow front bencher and the person who came second in the Tory leadership contest to replace Rishi Sunak.[240] Jenrick criticised the Tories for the explosion in the rising costs of the welfare bill, partly due to five million migrants entering the country during the Tory government's reign in power, something that Rachel from accounts tried to fix but was defeated by her own backbenchers. Jenrick would also abolish the Home Office in its current form. My response about time someone tackled defunct bureaucracy and replaced it with a new borders department whose major responsibility would be to stop the small boat crossings.[241] In my opinion, there aren't many small boats; some of them are huge, but I suppose in terms of Ocean liners, they are small. In fact, I would personally go further and stop funding any charity that supported illegal immigrants by providing mobile phones or funding for clothes and other supplies, but that is just my opinion.

A very encouraging and welcome consequence of Robert Jenrick's defection to Reform is that 22 percent of Conservative voters said they would follow Robert in switching to Reform.[242] However, it is important to point out that 54% of respondents in the survey stated the defection had no impact on their voting intention and 48 percent declaring the defection had not changed their mind.[243] I remain quite sceptical about the accuracy of small polls that include one thousand people out of the millions of UK voters. Sir Jacob Rees-Mogg came out after Robert Jenrick's defection and appealed that the

---

[240] Ben Riley-Smith, Tony Diver, Dominic Penna, Daniel Martin. Jenrick: Tories broke Britain. The Telegraph. 15 January 2026.
[241] Liam Halligan, Allison Pearson. Jenrick: I'd split up the 'not fit for purpose' Home Office. The Telegraph. 22 January 2026.
[242] Marcus Donaldson. One in 5 Britons more likely to vote Reform after Robert Jenrick defection, new polling reveals. GB News. 16 January 2026.
[243] Donaldson.

Conservatives and Reform UK unite in order to go into the next general election with a united right-wing-leaning party.[244] However, both Nigel Farage and Kemi Badenoch have ruled out any chance of a coalition, which, in my opinion, is the correct choice because the Tory coalition with the Liberal Democrats under David Cameron and Nick Clegg was a disaster. After Robert Jenrick, there is to date one final giant defection from the Conservatives to Reform UK, that of Suella Braverman.[245] The former home secretary was subject to defamatory comments from the Conservatives, which included a comment that Suella had mental health issues, an allegation which was clearly defamatory. Even if the accusation was correct, it is an unlawful disclosure of personal information contrary to the Data Protection Act 2018.[246]

London Mayoral Elections

Nigel Farage has pledged to restore law and order to London in 2026 and emphasised that lawlessness was the predominant issue in London. Crime is the biggest problem for London, with the closure of eighty percent of police stations in London since 2010. The problem in London is not just law and order, although crime is a dominant issue, but also the cost-of-living problems driven by mass migration into London.[247]A contributory factor is that eighty per cent of police stations have closed since 2010, and a police presence on the streets of London is almost invisible in every way. There is the well-recognised issue of knife crime in London and the escalating issue of mobile

[244] Dominic Penna. The right 'must unite' after Jenrick defection, urges Rees-Mogg. The Telegraph. 16 January 2026.
[245] Daniel Martin, Amy Gibbons, Genevieve Holl-Allen. Suella Braverman Defects to Reform. The Telegraph. 26 January 2026.
[246] Katie Harris, Reform UK threatens to sue Kemi Badenoch over Suella Braverman mental health claim. The Express 29 January 2026.
[247] Domonic Penna. Farage promises to restore law and order to London. The Telegraph. 1 January 2026.

phone thefts. While all 32 London Boroughs are due to hold local elections in May 2026, the Mayoral elections will not take place until 2028. This May, a total of 1,817 councillors in all London boroughs and the five mayors will be elected.[248]

The elections will be a profound test of Reform's credentials to win an outright majority in a general election. Indeed, Nigel Farage has described the London elections as the "single most significant" electoral test before the next general election.[249] Regardless of who wins control of the individual London Boroughs, they will have to deal with and overcome a massive £4.7 billion shortfall in collective budgets across London in the period up to 2029. The number of London Boroughs requiring exceptional financial support could rise from seven in 2025/26 to seventeen by 2028.[250]

The Reform UK candidate for the London mayoral elections in 2028 is Laila Cunningham, and she is campaigning under the auspices of "London needs Reform."[251] Laila will focus on a crackdown on crime and is coming with a "different message" for Londoners. The emphasis will be on the Metropolitan police force to tackle and reduce knife crime, drug abuse, robbery, shoplifting and rape. There will be a special emphasis on the police to hunt down and prosecute rape gangs within the capital. As is predictable, Laila, once announced as a Reform UK candidate face racial and misogynistic abuse online.[252] The battle lines are clearly drawn, and there is no doubt that failure is not an option.

---

[248] Tony Grew. 2026: Council tax hikes on the agenda as London votes. BBC News 1 January 2026.
[249] David Lynch. Who is Laila Cunningham? The Reform UK candidate for London mayor. The Independent. 15 January 2026.
[250] Tony Grew.
[251] David Lynch
[252] Jack Walters. Nigel Farage blasts 'nasty' racist abuse directed at Laila Cunningham but rejects calls for X ban. GB News. 10 January 2026.

Gorton and Denton By-Election February 2026

According to Allister Heath, British democracy is in its death throes due to the terror of the Gorton and Denton by-election.[253] The fear is that we are becoming a country where the race of the voter or religion of the voter determines who votes for which political party. Is Britain sleepwalking into becoming a Lebanon-on-Thames, or more realistically, a Lebanon-on-London, Manchester, Birmingham, or Rotherham?[254] Is the segregation of voters and MPs in the House of Commons going to reflect the segregation of the electorate? Jake Simons sees the Green Party election victory in Gorton as the most shameful and disturbing instance in British political history.[255]Simons refers to the Green Party campaign as weaponising sectarianism and bigotry. Are we experiencing the collapse of democratic norms, and what effect will it have on British politics going forward? Sectarianism is becoming an assured driver of British politics[256] . Simons predicts that there is more sectarianism, bigotry, anger, hatred, extremism and less democracy as Britain descends into the dark abyss.

Nigel Farage believes the Denton by-election was "a victory for sectarian voting and cheating,"[257] While Zach Polanski, the leader of the Green Party, believes the Gorton by-election result will transform the face of British politics and a vote for the Green Party is not a wasted vote.[258] Polanski predicts a 'tidal wave' of Green MPs at the next election, with the party aiming for more than 100 seats if the

---

[253] Allister Heath. The abominable by-election is a final warning for Britain's democracy. The Telegraph, 25 February 2026.
[254] Allister Heath.
[255] Jake Wallis Simons. The Greens' extremist victory pushes Britain one step closer to the abyss. The Telegraph, 27 February 2026.
[256] Simons.
[257] Nigel Farage, Farage: By-election was 'a victory for sectarian voting and cheating' The Telegraph, 27 February 2026.
[258] Zach Polanski: This victory will transform British politics. The Telegraph, 27 February 2026.

Gorton and Denton result is repeated throughout Britain.[259] Given how new political parties are lining up across Britain, maybe it is time for Reform UK to consider their strategy to overcome the Green Party, particularly?

The question remains whether this was a protest vote against the Labour Government or a turning point in British politics. Was it a major mistake by Starmer to block Andy Burnham from running in the Gorton by-election, as polls suggest that Burnham would have won 49 percent of the vote and, in all probability, retained the seat for Labour?[260] How big a disaster this by-election defeat for Labour will be will only be seen in the coming months and years, with the local council elections scheduled for 7 May 2026 and a general election no later than May 2029.

Is it too late to turn around the growing prejudices in British society driven by religious extremism? Is it time for Christians and Jews to abandon Britain and get out before they are driven out? The scariest question is whether Britain is heading to the kind of sectarian troubles that plagued Northern Ireland in the 1970s. Only time will tell. Whatever the outcome, it is clear that British political history has changed and not necessarily for the better.

Fallout

The projections from the Gorton by-election are that if the result were repeated throughout the country at the next general election, Reform UK would have a working majority in government, and the Green Party would be the official opposition. It is just a projection and has no basis in reality. However, it does leave open a role for Reform UK as the "radical centre right" of British politics, and there is room to

---

[259] James Bullen, Greg Heffer. Live update. Daily Mail, 27 February 2026.
[260] Dominic Penna. Labour 'to come third in key by-election.' The Telegraph, 20 February 2026.

drive home the importance of Reform's UK ideological policies. Reform UK will need to more strongly oppose Labour's Orwellian nightmare policies and, where possible, stop them altogether.[261] To own some of Dunt and Dorian's ideas, Reform UK must drive home that we are a new party with new radical ideas that are beneficial for the whole of Britain, not just the majority.[262] The Gorton by-election highlighted more than ever before that Britain is in a battle between good and evil and between right and wrong. Labour, the Lib Dems and the Green party have formed an axis of evil which aims to destroy the British way of life as we know it, either by making Britain a communist socialist state, or by surrendering power to the European Union or by a free-for-all approach of open borders for all, where immigrants, legal or illegal, prevail over the British people. A country that could degenerate into a sectarian, borderless, defenceless, drug-fuelled, lawless nation that has never been witnessed in the history of civilisation. Britain is broken, and only Reform UK recognise that fact and has the policies and direction to fix the problem.

Things to Overcome

In general, democracies have been dependent on economic performance and optimism about the future.[263] The biggest opposition to democracies is financial instability, prejudice and anxiety. Fear or anxiety about the future opens the door for totalitarian regimes that offer protection against an authentic or mythical or notional danger.[264] Citizens seek protection from multiple threats that are intrinsic in society, loss of money, economic insecurity, accidental injury, sickness,

---

[261] Ian Dunt, Dorian Lynskey. Page 83 in Centrism: The story of an idea. Weidenfeld & Nicholson, London, UK, 2024.
[262] Dunt & Dorian, page 85.
[263] Sumption, page 5.
[264] Sumption, page 6.

lawlessness, crime and sexual violence.[265] If governments find themselves accountable for all that fails in society, they will remove our freedom so that they are not accountable for anything.[266] Consequently, pressure groups can initiate what in real terms are terrorist assaults on democracy by insisting that only their views are correct on a variety of subjects, such as race, gender, same-sex relationships, immigration, etc. Those who fail to accept the campaigner's point of view are vilified or, in extreme cases, banned from the intellectual world.[267] For example, the institution of a Reform UK society by the Student Union at the University of Sussex led to widespread protests from the Green Society and anti-fascist groups.[268] The decision led to huge criticism from students, calling for the Reform Society to be discontinued due to the party's values and ideology. In a separate incident, Sarah Pochin, a sitting Reform UK MP and Jack Anderton, a Reform activist, were prevented from attending a question-and-answer session at Bangor University by Snowflake woke students.[269] Democracy can only survive if all differences of opinion are given an equal platform to debate their points of view.[270]

As Zia Yusef and Richard Tice pointed out, Bangor University receives £30 million of taxpayers' money, and if they don't want freedom of speech, then their funding should be removed, as many of the taxpayers who fund the university are members of Reform UK.[271]

---

265 Sumption, page 8.
266 Sumption, page 9.
267 Sumption, page 10.
268 Francesca Williams. University of Sussex Reform society receives backlash. The Argus, 31 January 2026.
269 Christine Calgie. Fury at woke university students ban Reform MP from debate over 'racism and transphobia,' The Express, 10 February 2026.
270 Sumption, page 10.
271 Christine Calgie.

Chapter 6:

What Are We Aiming for? General Principles and Direction

A Balanced Society

According to Danny Kruger, a happy society is an association of people with multiple things in common outside of themselves, resulting in a society of self-determining, self-moralising individuals. It is where the only thing held in common is humanity itself.[272]

The idea here is that you are what you worship. No one admits that the enemy is other people, or proudly declares their wish to subjugate everyone else to their own elitist worldview.[273] T The main principle of personal dignity and individual value is: I don't care what other people think. The Human Rights Act has the power of being sovereign and permanent, the equivalent of a constitutional document. It is immune to all subsequent laws. It also gives judges the power to amend earlier legislation to suit their doctrines.[274]

The court can modify the meaning, and therefore the context of the law, resulting in lawyers and judges becoming the power in the country.[275] The Equality Act of 2010 imposed a duty on public

---

[272]Danny Kruger, page 41. Covenant: The new politics of home, neighbourhood and nation. Forum Books, Croydon, UK, 2024.
[273] Kruger, page 42-43
[274]Kruger, page 49
[275]Kruger, page 50

agencies to eliminate unlawful racial discrimination. The dogma of a positive moral code that attempts to ensure that people from ethnic minorities are not specifically disadvantaged in the workings of the public sector. This moves people into the sphere of thought crime, as seen in this Labour government, where people silently praying outside of abortion clinics are arrested, and people who post certain things that the government don't like on social media are prosecuted.[276] According to the idea, the enemy is not within each of us, but out there in the ether of our thoughts. It is the other people and society itself that are the enemy.[277]

According to Kruger, ECHR, the Human Rights Act and the Equality Act should be amended, but simply replaced with simple assertions contained in the 1951 Convention and indeed many preceding statutes in English law, that the state shall protect the life, liberty and prosperity of its citizens and not interfere with them itself without due process.[278]

Kruger argues that rights properly should consist of legal protections against interference by government or others when people fulfil their everyday tasks and obligations.[279] Therefore, citizens require protection against false imprisonment, theft and mistreatment. Citizens should be free to speak, assemble and worship according to their inclination and conscience. Citizens require the ability to raise a family and to direct the education of their children, and should have the right to a trial by jury, overseen by judges who follow the statute and precedent, applying the law as they believe it to be, not as they think it should be.[280]

---

[276]Kruger, page 54
[277]Kruger, page 55
[278]Kruger, page 56
[279]Kruger, page 56
[280]Kruger, page 56-57

The Human Rights Act has given substantial authority to judges in Strasbourg and the High Court in London over pivotal questions related to national freedom of individuals, who, in many instances, the government believes should be removed from the UK.[281]

Human rights laws impinge on national sovereignty as the courts wrestle the power away from the government. The Human Rights Act does not prevent governments from imposing draconian laws which seriously infringe the right to freedom of speech. Human rights laws should not impact moral decisions such as stopping known terrorists, paedophiles, rapists and murderers from entering a country or remaining within that country.

These decisions should be made by the government, not by the courts. Human rights may provide the illusion that individuals are free to behave exactly as they wish without fear of deportation.[282] Gittos makes an important point when he asks if judges should be the bona fide establishment for safeguarding personal human rights and freedom, especially in the light of Stalin's attack on free speech, as he has been pointed out in numerous social media posts, especially the decision to limit trials by jury.[283] Human rights institutions have tried to rationalise the pursuit of overall morality under the aegis of the rights of the individual.[284]

Human rights laws have achieved mythical status in the UK, which is far from the reality that they protect a restricted concept of morality and freedom. The argument is that relying on a democratically elected government to determine the parameters of human rights would lead to totalitarianism and ultimately to genocide.[285] The bottom line is,

---

[281] Luke Gittos. Human rights-illusory freedom, page 2. Zero Books, Winchester, UK. 2018
[282] Gittos, page 9.
[283] Gittos, page17
[284] Gittos, page75
[285] Gittos, page93

what does freedom mean? Being free to commit acts of terror, knowing that you cannot be deported if you are returning to your country of birth to be executed. Likewise, should paedophiles, rapists and murderers be allowed to stay in the UK to escape justice in their home countries?[286]

Both Conservative and Labour governments have pitched for the undermining of human rights, but by stopping the right to silence and by stopping trials by jury for many offences, so any individual who refuses to defend himself is considered guilty until proven innocent. The Labour government is now introducing extensive, draconian laws to regulate and inhibit, in some instances, abolish freedom of speech by calling it a hate crime.[287] How do we respond when free speech is continually equated with violence and anarchy? Anybody objecting to immigration is labelled a racist.[288] It is easy to see the high level of vengeful remarks, especially on social media, when there are concerns of white British people to the level of immigration occurring in Britain.

The unforgiving nature is especially expressed by left-wing politicians. Particularly those associated with Reform UK were demonised for suggesting that those entering the country illegally should be sent back to their country of origin.

Gross Domestic Product

Nothing is more important for increasing people's standard of living than continued economic growth. Even modest changes in the growth rate, when sustained and maintained over extended periods of time, make a huge difference in the standard of living for UK citizens.[289]

---

[286] Gittos, page122
[287] Gittos, page 7.
[288] Murray, page 35.
[289] Lumen macroeconomics. The Power of Sustained Economic Growth. https://
courses.lumenlearning.com/wm-macroeconomics/chapter/components-of-economic-growth/

Gross domestic product (GDP) per capita is a key indicator of our nation's prosperity, and currently, the UK's GDP is slightly above pre-COVID-19 pandemic levels, and when it is adjusted for living costs, it is trailing behind many Western nations, including Italy.[290] When the economy is growing, then employment increases as there are more jobs to deal with the increased demand of production, as there is more income generated, salaries increase, and when salaries increase, there is more disposable income to fuel the economy. It is a cycle of expansion. However, increasing unemployment is an indication that the economy is slowing or heading for recession. Unemployment in the UK in January 2026 stands at 5.1%, which is the highest level for four years.[291] Within July to September 2025, the UK's GDP grew by 0.1% compared with April to June 2025, this compared to France with a 0.5% increase, Germany no growth and the USA grew by 1.1%.[292] The International Monetary Fund forecast that UK GDP would grow by 1,3% in 2026 and 1.5% in 2027.

As Starmer acknowledges, small levels of public and private investment have resulted in low growth and productivity. Our GDP per hour worked has only increased by 0.6% since 2010, while in Germany, France and the US, GDP has grown by around 1% a year during the same time period.[293] The UK has fallen behind other G7 countries in relation to business investment. Consequently, this has negatively impacted the development of new jobs, industries, and technology. However, this doesn't explain the increasing unemployment in the UK, which has been attributed to increased National Insurance on businesses and other taxes and an increase in

---

[290] McCowan, page 79.

[291] Office for National Statistics. Labour market overview, UK: December 2025

[292] GDP International comparisons. House of Commons library number 02784. 19 January 2026.

[293] Prime Minister's Office. Kickstarting Economic Growth. https://www.gov.uk/missions/economic-growth

the minimum wage, making employers reluctant to take on new workers; consequently, the job market has shrunk under Labour.

Economic Impact of Brexit

While I outlined the role of Brexit and the Labour government earlier, it is worth recapping here the background to the lies generated by the Conservatives in the REMAIN campaign and underlining here the truth regarding Brexit and the positive impact it has had on the economy. George Osborne's 87-page economic impact of leaving the EU analysis, published by HM Treasury on the effects of leaving the EU published on 23 May 2016, just one month before the referendum, predicted a doomsday scenario for the UK economy if the UK voted to leave.[294] It predicted that the UK economy would shrink by 6 percent within two years of Brexit, with an estimated increase in unemployment of 800,000.[295] In reality, the UK GDP rose by 4.2 percent by the second quarter of 2018, and unemployment fell by 306,000, as Ross Clark states the Treasury forecast was "laughable" and clearly way off the mark. It is obvious that the COVID pandemic had a major impact on economies across the globe, but despite this and an obvious stagnation of growth in the UK economy following Brexit in 2019 through 2023, the UK economic still showed an overall growth of 1.8% between Brexit in 2019 and the second quarter of 2023.[296] The UK continued to struggle into 2025, with GDP growth in the second and third quarter of 2025 was 0.3% and 0.1%, respectively, with a projected growth of 1.3% compared to the same period in 2024.[297] The UK GDP growth for the third quarter 2025, compared to

---

[294] George Osbourne. HM Treasury analysis: The immediate pact of leaving the EU.
[295] Ross Clark, page 12. In Far from Eutopia: How Europe is failing and Britain could do better. Abacus, London, UK 2025
[296] Ross Clark, page 12-13.
[297] Office of National Statistics. GDP first quarterly estimate, UK: July to September 2025.

the same period in 2024, was 1.3% this can be compared with 1.4% for the Eurozone, 2.3% for the USA, 0.7% for Japan, 0.3% for Germany and 0.9% for France.[298] While the economy is not doing as well as could be expected and there is a clear need for improvement and growth of the GDP, it has not been catastrophic or overtly apocalyptic.

What are the things that are inhibiting the GDP economic growth that the UK so desperately needs for sustainability, reducing unemployment and improving the quality of life of its citizens? Clark suggests that fanatical, stupid net-zero targets throughout Europe are responsible for influencing large companies to move to other regions of the world.[299] Despite constant claims by Ed Miliband that renewable energy and net zero are the best thing since sliced bread and that wind and solar energy are going to create thousands of jobs and save consumers massive amounts in their energy bills, the opposite has happened, which has left the UK with the highest energy bills in Europe. In terms of wind energy, I do side very much with Donald Trump's opinion, "China doesn't use windmills for energy. They use coal. They build windmills and sell them to stupid people." It is interesting to note that wind turbines are sometimes stopped, firstly due to a lack of wind to enable them to be switched on, but also, conversely, due to too much wind. Excessive wind speeds of excess of 90 km/hr are considered dangerous for the wind turbine, and therefore they are shut down for their own safety.[300]

If a Reform UK government are to reduce energy costs in order to stimulate investment in the UK and kick start industrialisation, then

---

[298] House of Commons Library. GDP International comparisons: Economic Indicative. 19 January 2026.
[299] Ross Clark, page 21.
[300] Endesa.com. Why do we see wind turbines stopped if there is enough wind? 27 January 2026. https:// www.endesa.com/en/the-e-face/energy-sector/wind-turbines-stopped-with-wind

they need to stop stupid net zero, a policy that is high on the list of objectives. Reform UK will scrap net zero to cut energy bills and restore growth; scrap £10 billion of government renewable energy subsidies; fast-track cheaper, more secure domestic energy production; support cleaner, more reliable nuclear and tidal power; and incentivise cleaner energy from new technologies. A common-sense approach at last. A cautionary note regarding the building of nuclear power stations, it is well documented that the problems associated with the building of the power station at Hinkley and the escalating costs associated with the building of the power station.[301] On average, it takes 25 years to go from the planning stage to completion, which means it is more of a long-term fix than a short-term answer to cheap energy prices.

Brexit and Reform UK

There is little doubt that Brexit caused huge changes to the UK's trade with the EU, with the exit from the single market and customs union, and this was replaced by the Trade and Cooperation Agreement (TCA).[302] The impact of Brexit has so far had very little impact on overall UK trade, although moving to the TCA has resulted in a small reduction in exports to the EU and consequently, many importers have changed their policy to trading within the UK or from non-EU countries.[303] It is clear that to date, UK trade has become more adaptable than critics predicted.

What has Brexit achieved? The vote to leave the European Union aimed to restore the UK's freedom for self-government to be free at

---

[301] Ross Clark, page 27.
[302] Dennis Novy, Thomas Sampson, Catherine Thomas. Brexit and UK trade. Centre for Economic Performance. Paper number CEPEA058. June 2024.
[303] Novy, et al. page 1.

last to make our own laws and decisions free from interference by Brussels.[304] Our freedom should allow us to negotiate our own trade deals, amend our laws to increase benefits to British citizens and draw closer to non-EU countries. The biggest fallacy and misconception in staying in the EU was that the single market is crucial to the economic wellbeing of the UK.[305]

If the UK had remained a member of the EU, which both Labour and the Liberal Democrats have called for, the UK would have been the second-largest funder of its £650 billion budget for 2021-2024. The UK contribution would have been £88 billion. This puts into perspective the Labour Government's imaginary "£22bn black hole" by a factor of four, and the UK would have been faced with a funding gap that was five times higher than the one supposedly inherited by Rachel from accounts.[306] If Brexit was done properly and not botched in red tape, then Brexit should have brought us benefits by saving us billions of pounds sterling in EU fees and membership costs, it should have returned our independence in fishing, farming, animal welfare and the environment, something the Labour Government is determined to destroy. Brexit means better trade with non-EU countries. More importantly, we run our own country again.[307] Brexit improves the economy, and if implemented correctly, Brexit should enable the UK to control its own borders.[308] Finally, Brexit has improved the UK's standing in the world. This can be seen by our current trade figures. In 2024, the UK exported £868 billion of commodities and services and imported £897 billion, resulting in a

---

[304] John Redword, page1. In Gully Foyle 75 BREXIT benefits. Bruges Group Publications, London, UK 2025

[305] John Redword, page 2.

[306] BREXIT Facts4you.org. REVEALED: How Brexit actually saved Rachel from a £110bn 'black hole' Rachel Reeves' "£22bn black hole" would have been dwarfed by £88bn paid by UK to EU.
Https://www.facts4eu.org/news/2025_oct_rachel_saved_by_brexit#

[307] Foyle, page 12.

[308] Foyle, page 13.

trade deficit of £29 billion.[309] Closer scrutiny showed that the UK exported £358 billion of goods to the EU in 2024, which accounted for 41.2% of UK trade, but imported £454 billion of goods from the EU, which accounted for 50.6% of UK trade. Trade between the UK and the EU resulted in a £96 billion deficit.[310] This can be compared with £510 billion exports the UK made to non-EU countries and £443 billion imports from non-EU countries a £67 billion profit. So, 58.8% of UK exports went to non-EU countries compared with 49.4% of imports. These figures show that trading with non-EU countries is profitable while trading with the EU is detrimental to the UK economy. A closer look at UK trade in goods between the UK and the EU shows a deficit of exports versus imports for every single year since 2010. The deficits between exports and imports between the UK and the EU grew each year between 2010 and 2016, accounting for the pre-Brexit years. (2010 -£32 billion, 2011 -£34 billion, 2012 -£56 billion, 2013 -£68 billion, 2014 -£75 billion, 2015 -£83 billion and 2016 -£90 billion).[311]

However, Starmer is trying to form closer ties with Brussels and sell the UK's independence back to Brussels in an open betrayal of democracy.[312] Already, Starmer has made a fisheries agreement with the EU, granting EU fishermen to fish in the UK waters and extending the current deal until 2038 in a betrayal of the UK fishing industry.[313] Critics have branded Keir Starmer's fishing deal with the EU "a horror show" for the industry after he granted European trawler fleets 12 years of access to UK waters. The rollover of the existing fisheries deal

---

[309] Domonic Webb, Matthew Ward. Page 7. House of Commons Library. Statistics on UK trade with the EU. 22 April 2025

[310] Domonic Webb, Matthew Ward, page 7.

[311] Domonic Webb, Matthew Ward, page 12

[312] Peter Foster, George Parker, Anna Gross, Andy Bounds. EU demands 'Farage clause' as part of Brexit reset talks with Britain. Financial Times. 11 January 2026

[313] Alicja Hagopian. In charts: What does the new Brexit deal mean for fishing? The Independent. 20 May 2025

to 2038. Starmer is also aligning the UK's food and agriculture with the EU's single market in a betrayal of Brexit and a capitulation to the EU.[314]

The EU is afraid that any future Reform government would reverse any agreements that Starmer has made with the EU. As a consequence, the EU are insisting that any future UK government pays significant financial compensation if they quit a post-Brexit UK-EU deal. The EU has included a termination clause that would require the UK to pay a substantial level of compensation if it withdraws from any EU agreement and has labelled the fine as a "Farage clause," which they hope will ensure that any future Reform UK government would find it difficult to reverse Starmer's betrayal of Brexit.[315]

The challenge for a new Reform UK government is how to proceed with our relations with the EU post-Brexit. Will there be some form of trade-off in order to increase the much-needed increase in UK productivity and the associated improvement in employment and standards of living?[316] There is an obvious opportunity with increasing trade with the EU, given the close proximity of Europe to the UK, but any increase in trade with the EU needs to be beneficial to Britain and in line with the principles and spirit of Brexit.[317]

---

[314] Tom. The London Economic. Finally! Stamer slams broken Brexit promises – and eyes closer ties with EU single market. 4 January 2026.
[315] Foster, et al.
[316] Novy, et al. page 14.
[317] Novy, et al. page 14.

Chapter 7:

What Comes Next?

Core Pledges

A Reform UK government must deliver on its promises, and there can be no excuses. If elected, we have a mandate to reverse years and years of wastefulness and failure of both the Conservatives and the Labour Governments. The Reform UK core pledges include removing all illegal immigrants from Britain. Linked to this pledge is the promise to detain and deport all illegal migrants who came to the UK in small boats, and if necessary, intercept migrants coming in small boats in the English Channel and return them to France. This pledge is the one thing that has the Uniparties calling Reform supporters racist. Our membership has grown on a platform of restricting immigration and putting British people first before immigrants.[318] This will be an area where the high court and the ECHR will oppose the most, as the Labour Government are finding out at their cost.

Pro-immigrant lawyers have successfully managed to overturn even the vilest of immigrants due for deportation, such as paedophiles, murderers and rapists, usually on the grounds that they face far harsher sentences if returned to their countries of origin. There have been cases where the illegal immigrant is returned to their country of origin. However, Reform UK will have to implement the draft bills already prepared to ensure this does not occur, as the cost of failure on this pledge alone will incur the wrath of the electorate. Success in returning migrants to their original countries will have the knock-on effect of

---

[318] McCowan, page 32.

boosting wages for British citizens, protecting overstretched public services, reducing the housing crisis and cutting crime, as crimes carried out by foreign nationals account for nearly 80% of arrests for theft on Britain's trains and public transport. Data from the Centre for Migration Control (CMC) shows that 79.3% of theft-of-passenger-property arrests involved migrants during the 2024-2025 period.[319] Foreign nationals account for nearly 80% of arrests for theft on Britain's trains and public transport. Data from the Centre for Migration Control (CMC) shows that 79.3% of theft-of-passenger-property arrests involved migrants during the 2024-2025 period.

Furthermore, data from the CMC highlights the scale of the migrant crime crisis gripping the UK, with over 104,000 foreign national convictions taking place between 2021 and 2023.[320] These figures include 38,413 for violent crime, sexual assault, drug-related crime and theft. Shockingly, foreign nationals were convicted for sexual offences at a rate 71% higher than that of the British population, 69% higher for drug-related crime, 25% for theft, and at 39% higher for all crime types. The top five nationalities by conviction per 10,000 were: Albania, Moldova, Congo, Namibia, and Somalia. For sexual offences, people were predominantly from Afghanistan, Eritrea, Namibia, Chad, and Moldova. There were 87 nationalities with a higher conviction rate for sexual offences than the British population. In 2024, these nationalities were awarded 557,041 long-term visas by the Home Office.

If we take note of an ex-prime minister who failed spectacularly in just 44 days, then we must take seriously what any Reform Government

---

[319] Ciaran McGrath. Outrage as non-Brits make up 80% of offenders behind 1 UK crime. Express online 17 January 2026.
[320] Centre for Migration Control. Over 100,000 foreign national convictions in just 3 years March 10, 2025. https://www.migrationcentral.co.uk/p/over-100000-foreign-national-convictions

would face when she states, the main obstacle in government is the sheer power of the administrative state and its influence on markets and the wider political organisation.[321] In government, there is a choice: go along with the orthodoxy or get booted out. In the current political system, we have unaccountable institutions that are more powerful than elected politicians and that pose a fundamental problem for parties across the political spectrum that seek to challenge the current dogma and status quo.[322]

The problem in the political establishment, driven by short-term popularity, drifting on prevailing winds of fashionable commentary, the real deep-rooted issues in our society and our world are considered too intractable to be tackled.[323] Again, the press in the UK has to be held accountable for this position, because from day 1 any new government will be under intense scrutiny with social media posts, particularly looking for failure or anything that can be manipulated as failure.

It is the job of the political leaders to lead. Britain needs leaders with the courage to put our country first. British people will come first under a reformed government. We are not the world's food bank. Welfare for British citizens only. We can recognise the warning signs of far-right extremism according to popular culture.

One key area where Reform UK has already made headway through local councils in their control is reducing unnecessary expenditure, and this can be extended to cover all of the whole country. For example, the Tories spent £230 billion in real terms on foreign aid over their 14 years to fund such abominations as a sex chatbot in Kenya, pay-as-you-chill coal storage in Zambia, and a 52-million road right through

---

[321] Truss, page 255.
[322] Truss page 275.
[323] Truss, page 16.

the Amazon to nowhere other than a tiny village in Guwana. All while the British people are taxed more than at any time in the last 80 years, and our public services stand on the brink of collapse. We need an end to this treachery and a full accounting of where all this money went, with consequences for fraud and theft. That is what reform will deliver, Zia Yusuf, Post on X on 31st December 2025.

Other key pledges from Reform UK include the pledge to reform the National Health Service to improve outcomes and to reduce waiting lists. More money needs to be directed toward patient care and less toward administration or exporting services to expensive private companies. It is important to reiterate that under Reform UK, the NHS will be free to all UK citizens, non-citizens will have to pay, and Reform UK will not privatise the NHS. In addition, Reform UK will provide tax relief of 20 percent for those patients who want to take out private medical insurance. Those who rely on the NHS will get faster, more reliable and better care.[324]

Reform UK pledge that good wages will be paid for a hard day's work and they plan to lift the income tax threshold to £20,000, which is aimed to save the lowest paid worker £1500 per year. This pledge will enable 7 million people to be taken off the need to pay any income tax and will be an incentive to take people off benefits.

However, the Centre for Policy Studies (CPS) reported that under the indefinite leave to remain (ILR) policies, between January 2021 and June 2024, just over 2 million visas were issued to migrants who will be eligible to apply for ILR in the UK.[325] The first of these migrants will be qualify for ILR from January 2026, at which point they will have

---

[324] Reform UK. Our contract with you, 2024.
[325] Karl Williams. Centre for policy studies. Recent migration wave may cost country billions, warns CPS. 9 February 2025

access to the NHS, social housing and Universal Credit. After 10 years of paying National Insurance, those with an ILR qualify for the state pension. It is estimated that somewhere between 742,000 and 1,224,000 migrants are likely to be granted ILR in the coming years. The CPs estimate that the lifetime net fiscal cost is £234 billion – equivalent to a bill of £8,200 for every UK household, spread out over several decades. However, it could be considerably more. Reform UK have pledged to overhaul the IRL system and to reduce the considerable tax burden on the country.

Reform UK has pledged to scrap the wasteful, stupid net-zero policies of the Labour Government, provide affordable, stable energy bills and save each household £500 per year. Linked to this policy, Reform UK will unlock Britain's vast oil and gas reserves to beat the cost-of-living crisis and to unleash real economic growth.

A Reform UK government must reverse the trend of 'non-doms' leaving Britain to date. 11,000 non-doms have already left the country in despair, and over a quarter of a million hard-working British citizens have upped sticks since Labour came to power.[326]

Specific Reform Policies

It is worth looking in more detail at specific Reform UK policies because these are the very policies and pledges that the Reform UK government will be held accountable for.

---

[326] David Bull. Reform members weekly bulletin 25 November 2025.

Reform UK Energy Policy[327]

Reform UK will reduce electricity costs by 30 percent by cancelling the green levies and the excessive de-carbonisation costs in the policy under the Labour government. Reform UK will rescind all net-zero legislation, encompassing the Climate Change Act of 2008, including the 2019 amendment and the 2023 energy bill. Reform will withdraw all pressure on homeowners to become more energy efficient. Reform UK will safeguard energy by leveraging the UK's own energy resources, like North Sea gas. Reform UK will provide accessible, competitive, dependable and protected energy supplies for all households across Britain, which will be compatible with elevated environmental principles. Coupled with net zero is the stupidity of the shutdown of two steel blast furnaces in Port Talbot in 2024.[328] The closure will reduce Britain's carbon emissions by 1.5 percent but it will have no impact globally because Britain will have to import steel from abroad, probably from China, although the USA under Donald Trump may be an alternative source of steel.[329] Also, closing the furnaces further reduces the UK's industrialisation and results in the loss of thousands of jobs and skills necessary to make steel.

Developing Industry[330]

Reform UK are the only political party that recognises the urgent need to protect and develop industry in the UK in order to create jobs and compete on the global stage. Over recent years industry in the UK has declined, and it is predicted that some industries, such as the chemical industry, which used to be a thriving industry both in the UK and

---

[327] Reform UK policies at Reform UK policy page 2026.
[328] Ross Clark, page 147.
[329] Ross Clark, page 147.
[330] Reform UK policies at Reform UK policy page 2026.

across Europe, will cease to exist in the next 20 years.[331] For example, Sir Jim Ratcliffe has pulled £3 billion of British investment through his energy empire Ineos due to taxes on North Sea oil and gas production imposed by Starmer's Labour governments. Ratcliffe has blamed high costs, such as the windfall tax and a levy on oil companies making massive profits, for the move. Ratcliffe will now move Ineos's investment to the USA.[332] This will have a knock-on effect of loss of jobs in the UK, but also the loss of an important industry and the loss of much-needed further investment in the UK. British businesses should not be deprived of their competitiveness in Britain. Reform UK will prioritise British firms in procurement, remove unnecessary regulation, and create a level playing field. It is clear that when British businesses succeed, Britain succeeds. Furthermore, the UK has the ability to lead the next wave of global innovation, but instead of adopting new technologies, political parties are suppressing them out of continuity, leaving Britain falling behind.

Reform UK will revitalise the British manufacturing industry so that it can once again become the workshop of the world. Domestic manufacturing will be supported through cheaper energy and easier regulation that favours British producers over foreign competitors. More manufacturing jobs will be created by ensuring that young people have the trained skills required to ensure success, and enabling them to participate with well paid jobs. It is obvious that a strong manufacturing industry will boost the UK economy. There are no well-paid jobs without thriving businesses, so Britain must be attractive to entrepreneurs. This can be achieved by cutting red tape, reducing business taxes, simplifying planning, and creating a stable, pro-enterprise environment. British workers will be given preference over

---

[331] Ross Clark, page 149.
[332] Charlie Herbert. Brexiteer Jim Ratcliffe abandons £3bn UK investment. The London Economic. 9 September 2025

foreign cheap labour. Reform UK policies will include an industrial strategy that ensures training and apprenticeships in order to create opportunities for British workers, especially young people.

Reform UK aims to establish Britain as a world leader in emerging technologies, including artificial intelligence, life sciences, advances in manufacturing and digital assets. Reform UK will create a pro-innovation regulatory environment that inspires and stimulates experimentation, commends investment, and entices the world's elite talent. Under Reform, technology will serve the British people, raise productivity, create high-paid jobs and enable progress, not hold it back.

Schemes and Targets[333]

The Reform UK manifesto lists a number of schemes and targets that Reform will implement when it becomes the next government in the UK. The much welcomed increasing the UK income tax threshold to £20,000 from the current £12,500, which has been frozen until 2031 by the Labour government. Coupled with Reform UK would scrap VAT on energy bills and lower fuel duty. Reform UK will reduce corporation tax to 20% abolish business rates for small and medium businesses on the high street. Introduce life skill classes at school for pupils and scrap interest on student loans. Increase the farming budget to £3 billion and increase UK food production to 70 percent as well as introducing subsidised agriculture apprenticeships. Retain the NHS workforce by scrapping student fees for doctors and nurses who have worked in the NHS for 10 years. Reform UK will reduce crime by hiring 40,000 new front-line police officers, and will increase defence spending to 2.5 percent GDP, and they will also increase the basic pay for personnel in the armed forces. All Reform UK tax cuts and

---

[333] Reform UK policies at Reform UK policy page 2026.

additional spending will be funded by reducing government waste without touching frontline services, which will provide potential savings of £156 billion while recognising that the cost of tax cuts amounts to approximately £141 billion.

Other measures that a Reform UK government will introduce are immediate deportation for foreign criminals and illegal immigrants, and they will introduce an offshore system to process migrants and return those who have entered the country by small boats to France. Reform UK will leave the ECHR and introduce a British bill of rights. Reform UK will fast-track new housing on Brownfield sites and prioritise social housing for British people ahead of migrants. Reform UK will also scrap net zero and fast-track new North Sea oil and gas licences, making the UK more energy dependent on energy created in the UK and not imported energy. Perhaps most welcome would be a Reform UK initiative to create jobs and get people back to work instead of being dependent on government benefits. The incentive to find work will include the proviso that job seekers must find work within 4 months; benefits will be withdrawn.

Restoring Justice[334]

Reform UK are developing strategies to tackle the key challenges facing the UK and has, for example, developed an "Operation Restoring Justice" plan, which is a plan to deport all illegal migrants in the UK and secure the UK's borders.[335] Reform UK recognise that over three decades, successive governments have promised to tackle illegal immigration into the UK, yet have spectacularly failed, with the estimated number of people with no right to remain in the UK standing at over one million people. This failure has several major

[334] Reform UK policies at Reform UK policy page 2026.
[335] Reform UK. Operation Restoring Justice: Our plan to deport illegal migrants in the UK, and secure our borders. Reform UK August 2025.

impacts by eroding the law on immigration, resulting in millions of pounds to support the costs of having these people in our country through providing accommodation, adding to a ballooning and unsustainable welfare budget and distorting the low-income labour job industry. It also makes the UK an attractive destination for illegal immigrants. Reform UK have a 5-year emergency plan that will result in the rapid deportation of all illegal immigrants, and will discourage any future influx of migrants by showing that illegal presence in the UK will be dealt with by their swift removal from the UK. It is estimated that this programme will save the UK taxpayer over £7 billion in the first five years and £42 billion in the first decade. Everyone deported because they have entered the country illegally will be banned from re-entering for life. One tactic that has been used by illegal immigrants has been the destruction of their identification, and under A Reform UK government, this will become a serious criminal offence. The outcome of the Reform UK plan is that the UK will once again become a sovereign nation with complete control over its borders.

It is reassuring to know that in a country that feels unsafe and is getting worse day by day, Reform UK aim to tackle this growing problem by making law-abiding citizens feel safer in their own country. Reform UK will achieve this by increasing visible policing, by delivering stronger sentences for serious and repeat offenders - including mandatory minimums, and a rigorous strategy to address offences and antisocial behaviour. Reform UK will increase stop and search approaches to remove deadly weapons from the streets of the UK. They plan to build more prisons to increase the number of prison places and to ensure violent criminals get the sentences they deserve, and they will ensure that there will be no early releases. Reform UK plans to create 12,400 new prison places on Ministry of Defence land in the first 18 months of being in power and to create 10,400 more prison places by transferring foreign national inmates to their country of origin.

They will bring in legislation to ensure that judges and courts enforce stern sentences, with the concept that the law will protect the law-abiding citizens but punish offenders. Victims will be first and not the criminals. Reform UK will endeavour to protect its citizens and ensure that safer streets are the foundation of the UK society. Coupled with this, Reform UK will rebuild Britain's armed forces, invest in capability and readiness, and restore morale across the intelligence and military services. They will ensure our armed forces are ready to deal with the ever-present threats posed by Russia and China. Subsequently, Britain will again earn the respect of our allies and be dreaded by our enemies and adversaries.

British Culture And Traditions[336]

A Reform UK government will protect British culture and traditions because these are a strong source of pride and unity. Reform UK will defend free speech, uphold British traditions, ban diversity, equity and inclusion quotas, and reject the politics of guilt. Reform UK will ensure British children are not indoctrinated in schools, that they learn British history and that religious freedom will remain a core feature of what the country is built upon, with the recognition that British culture is built upon Christian values, which will be protected under Reform UK.

Pubs are closing at an alarming rate - something like one a day closes, and which the Labour government are driving to oblivion, possibly by the need to appease their Muslim voters who want to abolish the sale of alcohol. Reform UK have stepped in with a plan and is the only

---

[336] Reform UK policies at Reform UK policy page 2026.

political party to do so. The Reform UK plan involves reducing the price of a pint by around £1 by the end of the next Parliament.[337] This will be achieved by reducing VAT to 10% for the hospitality sector. Reversing Labour's disastrous National Insurance hike on hospitality businesses - bringing it down from 15% to 13.8%, cutting beer duty by 10% and delivering a staggered abolition of business rates for all pubs.

When a pub closes in a rural community, it decimates the social fabric. The damage done is economic through lost jobs and reduced trade for nearby businesses, but also social, affecting people's health and wellbeing.[338] For some, especially those who live alone or are older, a visit to the pub is their main or even only chance to socialise and feel connected to others. This Labour government simply doesn't understand the pressure the sector is under. Reform UK does.[339]

Other Considerations

National Debt

Coupled with more efficient expenditure and reducing foolish expenditure, without doubt, the single biggest problem facing any new government is how to reduce the national debt. The UK's rising debt-to-GDP ratio is due to the country's abundant spending and borrowing, which greatly outweighs earnings.[340] According to Commodity.com, the UK national debt stood at 129.5% of GDP on 21 January 2026 and is increasing every second of the day. Currently, our debt stands at £2.9 trillion but is expected to pass £3.0 trillion in 2026. This problem didn't start under Starmer's government, although

---

337 David Bull, weekly newsletter to Reform UK members, 8 February 2026.
338 David Bull, 8 February 2026.
339 David Bull, 8 February 2026.
340 Read more at: https://commodity.com/data/uk/debt-clock/

Rachel from accounts has accelerated it. The problem of national debt began under Blair's government and was not dealt with under successive governments since. The beginning of the problem was the UK's debt-to-GDP spike, which started 1 year before the 2008 financial crisis — the figure more than doubled from 53.1% in 2007 to 107.4% in 2012.[341] A main theme of the rise of Reform is that Britain is broken, and this is true on so many different fronts, but most importantly in the area of the economy. A question raised by Adam McCowan is Britain's economy broken?

Britain's economy has stagnated since the financial crisis of 2008 and has consistently shrunk across all sections of the economy, with dire consequences as Britain's businesses are not able to expand as quickly as Western competitors.[342] There has been a catastrophic underinvestment in new technologies and the new skills required to compete with overseas competitors.

Trade

Reform UK will back those who take risks and those who create wealth to ensure that Britain is open for business.[343] There are critical reforms needed to stimulate business growth in the first 100 days of being in government. Reform UK will free over 1.2 million small and medium-sized businesses from corporation tax. They will also lift the minimum profit threshold to £100,000, reduce the main corporation tax rate from 25 percent to 20 percent and then to 15 percent in the third year of government.

---

[341] Commodity.com
[342] Adam McCowan. Is Britain's economy broken? Page 1. Self-Publication 2025.
[343] Reform UK. Our contract with you, 2024.

Reform UK will abolish the IR35 rules to support sole traders as Britain's self-employed work long hours and take more risks. Many sole traders have no pension and receive no sick pay. Reform UK will lift the VAT threshold to £150,000 to free up small entrepreneurs from red tape.[344]

The next step is to support small and medium-sized businesses by abolishing business rates, and the value of this will be paid for by an online tax dispensation plan set at 4 percent for large multinational companies and then cut entrepreneurs' tax to 4 percent. Reform UK would discard the plethora of laws that prevent British businesses from being competitive. They will also simplify employment laws to facilitate the growth of British businesses. Reform UK will also simplify the tax codes to make it easier for businesses.

Freedom

The major concern of a new Reform UK government must be the impact that immigration has on national security. Even with the promise to remove all illegal immigrants from Britain, this is going to take time, and it will be opposed by the far left and Lib Dems. The concern must be that the forced deportation of illegal immigrants could result in violent demonstrations and or terrorist attacks similar to the 7/7 terrorist attacks on London. Does Reform UK employ a last-in-first-out policy, or do they start by removing those who have been here the longest? Another conundrum is how to track down the many thousands that have simply disappeared and are in hiding. Implementation of policies that stop payments to illegal immigrants and remove housing, and especially if Halal practices were prohibited, then the incentive to stay in Britain would be far less attractive, and hopefully this would entice illegal immigrants to go back to France of

---

[344] Reform UK. Our contract with you, 2024.

their own accord. A further incentive to leave may be to remove the right to legal aid for those who entered the country illegally. However, the biggest obstacle would still be the attempts of judges in the UK High Court and ECHR lawyers trying to protect the rights of illegal immigrants at the expense of British citizens.

Freedom of speech must be restored for all with a redrafting of the 2023 online safety act so that people can express valid opinions without fear of being arrested or prosecuted because the government doesn't like what they said.

Fear for The Future

Throughout history, fear has been the primary device of the autocratic dominion.[345] Leaders hold a position of power or influence. Those who lead inspire us.[346] Capitalist societies will almost certainly experience reduced demand for products because there are just not enough people with enough money to buy enough products.[347] In these periods, it will be necessary to reduce interest rates so that businesses can borrow and invest more money, and consumers will have more excess cash to purchase items. The rationale behind why humans thrive is not because we are the most powerful, but because of our capacity to develop cultures.[348] Societies consist of a mass of folks who are joined by a collective fixed base of principles, values and beliefs.[349]The principles set down by society enable people to feel secure in the foundations of their beliefs. Multiculturism challenges the beliefs and principles of the society in which they are invading, and in extreme forms, the values of society that they wish to replace with their

---

[345] Sumption, page 46.
[346] Simon Sinek, dedication in Start with Why. Penguin Books, London, UK, 2025 edition.
[347] Ian Dunt, Dorian Lynskey. Page 53 in Centrism: The story of an idea. Weidenfeld & Nicholson, London, UK, 2024.
[348] Sinek, page 88-89.
[349] Sinek, page 89.

own views. When sufficient people from a different culture immigrate into the sphere of an existing culture, then it becomes an invasion. The outcome of the invasion is that the victor or stronger group who prevail will instil their beliefs in the weaker group, who may be enslaved in order to survive. Therefore, currently in 2026, there is a battle to preserve the Christian values upon which Britain was founded. As Sinek states, we are companions with individuals whose views of the world match our own.[350]

When assessing how immigrants fit into the values and beliefs of a community, they may end up as outcasts in the society they try to infiltrate and therefore are not productive. What happens to the members of society who are not contributing is at the centre of the discontent in Britain. Those who work for a living and pay taxes are rightly resentful towards those who are receiving more than them in social security and universal credit payments. The question is raised why I am struggling to make ends meet when others are viewed as merely scroungers because they have a better life and don't work to achieve it. The problem becomes toxic and worse when the scroungers are protected by a flawed ideology that seeks to protect the unemployed for the political gain of receiving their votes to maintain power. Under socialism, people rely too much on the state rather than on themselves, and this approach needs to radically change.[351] The prevailing ideology sees everyone who opposes it as racist, but in doing so, they lose perspective on the cost that their ideology is having on those who pay taxes in order to keep the country from desolation and destruction. It is clear that multiculturalism doesn't work, and those who have lived in Britain for generations are being driven out of their

---

[350] Sinek, page 89.
[351] James Davies, page 22 in Sedated: How modern capitalism created our mental health crisis. Atlantic Books, London, UK, 2022.

country by invaders from a different culture. It is clear that Britain is crumbling from within.[352]

The more Islam there is in society, the more hatred there is towards Islam.[353] We see thousands on the streets praying, most notably in areas of national importance, such as Parliament Square. They are not there to support the government but to demonstrate against it and show they are coming to overthrow the government. We have seen thousands taking to the streets in mass protest and can see that these protests often lead to violence, but this is just the beginning of what is about to occur as one culture invades another and seeks to overthrow the existing regime. We see that the alarm has been sounded against those who want to break up Britain or overthrow it.[354] What we see is a boiling cauldron below the surface, which at some point will explode into a volcano of overwhelming activity, and I fear great violence that has never been experienced within Britain outside of the Second World War.

The biggest enemies to the future of Britain lie within our borders and seek to overthrow the existing history of Britain and replace it with a new culture that is both foreign and aggressive against all who oppose it. The question that needs to be urgently answered is "Has Britain gone beyond the point of no return?" If we haven't passed the point of no return, we are teetering on the precipice that leads to the ultimate destruction of British society as we know it.[355] What is required to reverse the trend is a revival of gigantic proportions to return to our Christian roots before it is too late and all is lost. Russia and China are living proof that Socialism envisaged by the Fabian Society does not work for the majority of the population, and the massacre of citizens

---

[352] David E Gardner, page 65 in: The trumpet sounds for Britain volume 3. Christian Foundation Publications, Southend on Sea, UK, 2003.
[353] Murray, page 237.
[354] Gardner, page 71.
[355] Gardner, page 75.

wherever radical Islam reigns, such as Iran, Syria and Nigeria, shows that those who oppose it are slaughtered. Beware, Britain, what you hope for because you may well inherit a leviathan of massive proportions.

What we are seeing in Britain today is that the Christian values and culture of Britain is insidiously being taken from us, ward by ward and borough by borough. It is not an exaggeration to say that we are fighting for our very existence as a country. Yet, most people are not seeing or understanding what is happening, and I fear that they will not open their eyes to the truth until it is too late to rectify the problem. Churchill gave a once-famous speech that proclaimed:

We shall fight with growing confidence and growing strength in the air, we shall defend our Island, whatever the cost may be,

We shall fight on the beaches,

We shall fight on the landing grounds,

We shall fight in the fields and in the streets,

We shall fight in the hills;

We shall never surrender.[356]

Do we have the collective energy and desire to oppose what is happening on our beaches each passing day? I have my doubts.

---

[356] Winston Churchill. We shall fight them on the beaches. 4 June 1940. Full speech available at: Winston Churchill – We Shall Fight on the Beaches | Genius

Abortions

At present, I am unaware of any Reform UK regarding abortions in the UK, but I believe it is an important moral area that must be addressed. Sobering new figures released in January 2026 by the Department of Health and Social Care reveal that 278,740 abortions took place in England and Wales in 2023, the highest number ever recorded in a single year. Compared with the 252,122 abortions in 2022, the new figures represent an 11% rise, amounting to 26,618 additional lives lost to abortion in just one year. When combined with the record 18,242 abortions in Scotland in 2023 and the evidence-based estimate of 2,632 abortions in Northern Ireland in the same year, this brings the estimated total number of abortions across the UK in 2023 to 299,614, the highest figure ever recorded. 10,741,486 unborn babies have been aborted in the UK since 1968, when the Abortion Act 1967 came into effect.[357]

Sunday, 27 April marked 57 years since the abortion law came into force. At the current rate of abortion, according to the most recent figures, one baby is aborted every two minutes, and 31 babies' lives are terminated every hour. The number of abortions in England and Wales has reached a record high, with 252,122 taking place in 2022, while in Scotland, in 2023, there were a record 18,207 abortions, 1,600 more than in 2022, or a 9.63% increase from 16,607 in the previous year. This must be tackled as a matter of priority, and there must be ways to massively reduce the number of unwanted pregnancies and therefore reduce the number of abortions in the UK. Abortion should never be used as a final contraceptive, and better education and stronger abortion laws are required to combat this trend.

---

[357] Right to life. 57th anniversary of Abortion Act coming into effect, 10,741,486 lives lost since 1968. 25 April 2025

Chapter 8:

Local Issues

Why I Joined Reform UK

The simple answer to the question is that I joined Reform UK because of Nigel Farage. It was clear to me that the UK was in a mess in the last year of Sunak's Tory government and that things were out of control. I was totally uninterested in everything that Labour was saying, and their calls for change seemed to me false, and the claims that they were the party to put the country right appeared far from the truth. Ed Davey dressing up as a clown made me believe that if you vote for a clown, you get a clown. Also, the Lib Dem campaigners who turned up on my doorstep had one line vote Lib Dems if you want the Tories out. These same activists couldn't tell me what the Lib Dems actually stood for apart from opposing the Tory government. The 14 years of Tory failure, and especially Borisgate and Johnson's smirks at parliament when challenged about what he knew about the parties that were occurring at 10 Downing Street, made me angry because I could see the impact that the lockdown had on people who were barred from being with their loved ones in their final hours before passing. To my mind, this was criminal. During this period, I was looking for a party that reflected my views and had a clear vision for the UK, and every time I listened to Nigel, whether in television interviews or through social media, he was clearly a man with a vision and a direction I could identify with. It took me time because of the stigma that Reform UK were far right and racist, and this was, in the early days, a barrier. However, in June 2024, I joined because what Reform UK were preaching made sense. It was massively confirmed when I attended my first ever political conference in Birmingham, entitled Next Steps, in September 2025. I met so many people who shared the same views as me that the UK needed saving from the Uniparties. That there was a different way, and amongst the many people that I met from all over the country and from my local branch here in Wokingham, I haven't met a single person that could be called far right or racist. I haven't regretted joining and am very much looking forward to continuing the journey with Reform UK. I have very much appreciated the social media messages from Zia Yusuf, the weekly newsletter from David Bull and meeting Sarah Pochin and Jacob Rees Mogg at the 2025 Reform UK conference. The weekly meetings with colleagues and friends from the Wokingham Reform UK branch have all contributed to my journey. Not only do I feel welcomed and valued by Reform UK, but it is also, as Suella Braverman stated, a place to call home.

Immigration

When looking at local issues in Wokingham, immigration remains a concern, especially with an asylum hotel reopened in Wokingham in November 2024, with local residents having concerns about crime, anti-social behaviour and their safety. The opening of the asylum hotel coincides with the Lib Dems motion 502 brought by Caroline Smith, which recognised the potential contribution of asylum seekers and refugees to Wokingham, and they rashly believe that a coherent approach to elevate community adherence is the way forward to ensure the welfare of the people moving into Wokingham.[358] Notice it is to ensure the welfare of asylum seekers, not to protect the safety of the British residents of Wokingham. It is also noted that the Lib Dems welcome asylum seekers regardless of the way they arrived in the UK. This, in practical terms, means supporting unvetted illegal immigrants,

---

[358] Caroline Smith. Motion 502 submitted by Caroline Smith. Wokingham Borough Council. 20 July 2023. Available at: Agenda item - Motion 502 submitted by Caroline Smith | Wokingham

some of whom may be murderers, rapists, paedophiles or radical Muslims looking to introduce Sharia law in our community. The Lib Dems moved to make Wokingham a recognised 'Borough of Sanctuary' for asylum seekers. Furthermore, the Lib Dems are committed to actively seeking ways of supporting asylum seekers both within existing and future council tax budgets. This is at a time when people across the Borough are struggling to make ends meet and are having to cope with the highest taxation of any country throughout Europe. Also, focusing on asylum seekers above the council tax-paying residents of Wokingham results in the closure of social care programmes at a time when these budgets are already strained. It will put additional strain upon GP surgeries, dental practices, school places and social care housing. These issues are being fought nationally by Reform UK and also within Wokingham by the local branch.

Crime Rates

Crime and the safety of citizens are always at the top of everyone's list when considering both national and local issues. A poll of 1338 adults aged 18 – 30 years showed that 61 percent were worried about violent crime and revealed that young people feel increasingly unsafe in their own homes.[359] Specifically, knife crime has risen to near record levels in recent years, with well-published news items occurring on a regular basis to remind us of young lives being prematurely ended through violence. There has been a sustained reduction in violent crime over the last 10 years by 36 percent; however, there have been over a million incidents of violent crime recorded in the UK over this same period.[360] Nigel Farage is appalled by the state of violent crime in the UK and has pledged to invest in the police force and to enforce zero-tolerance

---

[359] Charles Hymas. Six in 10 young people fear becoming victims of violent crime. The Telegraph. 6 August 2025.
[360] Hymas.

policing, where the punishment fits the crime.[361] It is essential that no one should live in fear of violent crime or become a victim of violent crime. Despite reassurances that there is less crime, the British people remain unconvinced, and there is a fear that local communities will revert to vigilante groups.[362] The fear is that schools have become training grounds for violent criminals.[363] In 2025, there were 150 stabbings in schools in England and Wales, and over 20,000 violent crimes were reported in schools in 2024.[364] Moreover, between 2013 and 2023, there were 5,000 injuries to teachers caused by pupils. The problem of violence in society is undermined by the fact that often the perpetrators of violent crime are seen as victims and are handed nominal sentences or, in some instances, escape going to prison altogether and are allowed back on the streets to commit further atrocities and bring further heartbreak to their victims and their families.

Wokingham is not immune to violent crime, with one man being jailed for slashing the victim's face with a knife, as just a single example that violence occurs here in a small market town and isn't isolated in big cities.[365] The fact that there are potential problems in Wokingham schools can be highlighted by the fact that the police give talks in schools to prevent knife crime.[366] It is commendable to be pre-emptive, and prevention is always preferred to the consequences caused by the aftermath of any such horrors. So, how safe is Wokingham? As a snapshot of crime, there were 691 crimes reported

---

[361] Hymas.

[362] Isabel Oakeshott. It's no good telling us there's less crime. The British people know better. The Telegraph. 3 August 2025.

[363] Joe Baron. Schools have become training grounds for violent criminals. The Telegraph. 3 February 2026.

[364] Baron.

[365] Staff writer. Man jailed for slashing victim's face with knife in Wokingham. Wokingham Today. 9 February 2025.

[366] Staff writer. Wokingham police give talks in school to prevent knife crime. Bracknell News. 13 November 2024.

in Wokingham in October 2025, which were categorised into 14 different types.[367] The most commonly reported crime was violence and sexual offences, which were reported 253 (36.6%) of all crimes reported. This was followed by anti-social behaviour, accounting for 15.1 percent of all crimes. A closer look across Wokingham shows that in 2023, 2024 and 2025, violence and sexual crimes occurred 590 out of 2170 (27.2%), 544/1709 (31.8%) and 561/1624 (34.5%), respectively.[368] The worrying aspect of this is that violence and sexual crimes are increasing as a percentage of reported crimes and are the number one crime committed in Wokingham for each of these years. Anti-social behaviour and shoplifting also feature prominently as crimes committed in Wokingham between 2023 and 2025. While shoplifting figures are coming down for each year since 2023, anti-social behaviour remains a stable crime throughout the same time period.

According to Thames Valley police records, there were 22,015 violent and sexual offences committed in Wokingham between 2013 and 2022, with the highest number of crimes committed in 2019 and the lowest in 2014.[369] There were 21,838 anti-social crimes committed between 2010 and 2022, 11,455 criminal damage and arson crimes, 6859 shoplifting crimes reported in the same timeframe. Overall, the crime rate in Wokingham is 5.12 per 1000 of the population, which is lower than many areas of the UK, but is still worrying.

---

[367] Suzanne Antelm. Crime in Wokingham: the most common types revealed. Bracknell News. 7 January 2026.

[368] Thames Valley Police. Your local neighbourhood policing team. Available at Wokingham Town | Your area | Thames Valley Police | Thames Valley Police

[369] Crime Rate in Wokingham: Trends, Hotspots. CrimeTrends.co.uk Available at: Wokingham Crime Rate and Statistics

Solar Farms

The delivery of the Barkham Solar Farm in Wokingham is a key action of the Lib Dem council's climate emergency action plan in working towards a carbon neutral Borough.[370] By generating renewable energy locally and adding it to the local energy grid, the Lib Dems hope to reduce carbon emissions, secure sustainable power supplies, stabilise the costs of energy and help to reduce the cost-of-living crisis for residents in the long-term. However, as argued above, renewable energy has increased the cost of energy for every household in the UK, including those living in Wokingham. There is no sign that renewable energy will ever reduce energy bills for local residents. Indeed, energy bills rose in April 2025 by approximately 6 percent for each household in the UK. We have more renewable energy than ever before, yet the energy bills keep rising. This is due to the high upfront costs associated with developing renewable energy. Indeed, UK electricity prices are among the costliest in Europe and appreciably higher than those in the USA and Canada.[371] Retail gas prices are being blamed for the increases in household energy costs, which makes Reform UK's policy of developing our own North Sea gas very attractive indeed if it undoubtedly brings energy costs down.[372]

The local solar farm project in Wokingham will include the installation of approximately 43,000 solar panels and the associated equipment required for the functioning of the solar farm. The building of security fencing with sensor-controlled lighting and CCTV around the new perimeter.[373] Then there are the underground cables to connect the

---

[370] Wokingham Liberal Democrats manifesto 2024. Available at: Manifesto - Wokingham Liberal Democrats

[371] Marc Poynting, Anthony Reuben. If the UK has more renewable energy, why aren't bills coming down? BBC Verify. 24 April 2025.

[372] Emily Beament. Wholesale gas costs blamed for rises in household energy bills. The Independent. 28 January 2026.

[373] Wokingham Borough Council. Barkham solar farm project updated 8 January 2026.

energy generated from the farm to the national grid. This will require work on road carriageways and associated management of traffic. The cables will then have to be connected to an electricity substation. The costs of maintaining the solar farm are not mentioned, nor is it clear when the energy from the substation will be available to consumers. The costs for this project will be high and will be paid for by Wokingham council tax residents. It is clear that the Lib Dems won't meet their target of being online by Spring 2027, and costs for this project have soared to an estimated £28.6 million, funded through loans and leaving the council tax payers in Wokingham exposed to a further £3 million in interest rates.[374] The Lib Dems promise that the Solar farm will be beneficial for 40 years, but the average lifespan of the panels is only 25 years, meaning that they will have to be replaced as they reach the end of their lifespan at further cost to the Wokingham taxpayers.

As indicated above, net zero is doomed to failure unless everyone signs up and is committed to reducing their carbon footprint. As Tony Blair astutely put it, "The blunt truth about the politics of climate change is that no country will want to sacrifice its economy in order to meet this challenge." The better way to stop the build-up of greenhouse gases is to stop deforestation because trees are the best ally for capturing staggering amounts of carbon gases.[375] It is important to note just how important rainforests are in controlling carbon dioxide, the main culprit of greenhouse gases, as they act as a huge sponge that absorbs carbon dioxide. They also assist with rainfall by releasing oxygen into the atmosphere, which, when combined with hydrogen in the atmosphere, produces precipitation and thus also assists with

---

[374] Paul Creighton. Is the cost of making Wokingham home energy efficient worth it? Wokingham Today, 31 July 2023.
[375] Rainforest Alliance. What is the relationship between deforestation and climate change? 12 August 2018.

maintaining freshwater levels.[376] This has an associated effect of maintaining ecosystems and biodiversity. Trees have been labelled the lungs of the planet, and the process of photosynthesis is the foundation and cornerstone of life on Earth.[377]

Another approach to reduce carbon emissions and reduce increases of greenhouse gases into the atmosphere is the development of new technologies that elicit the burning of fossil fuels without releasing carbon.[378] Pre-combustion capture is a technology that converts fossil fuels into hydrogen and captures and burns the hydrogen and not the carbon. Also, there are initiatives with the capacity to remove greenhouse gases from the atmosphere, but these are expensive as experimental initiatives, like with all things, with time, the cost of these machines will reduce in price.[379] It is true to say that at this moment in time, I'm not aware of any political party that is seeking to invest in reforestation or new technologies for controlling carbon emissions, but with the insight that the leaders of Reform UK have, it may be a good direction to go in the near future.

Local Building Plans

Shortly after coming into power, the Labour government introduced its policy on housing targets to get Britain building again d to address the shortfall in affordable and social housing across the UK.[380] Within the plan, the government set new mandatory targets for local councils, with a review of greenbelt areas and trying to get these downloaded to 'grey belt' land and to drive a target of 50 percent of new homes

---

[376] Tony Orrowchild. Earth 2035, page 84. Authors Solution.co.uk. 2025.

[377] Alan E Shields. Page 40-41 In Deforestation exposed: trees, truths and tomorrow. Self-published. 2023.

[378] Orrowchild, page 83.

[379] Orrowchild, page 83.

[380] Ministry of housing, communities and local government, Angela Rayner MP. Housing targets increased to get Britain building again.Gov.UK 31 July 2024.

coming under the category of affordable housing. The target was to deliver 1.5 million new homes over a 5-year period. The government recognised that there was a need to develop new schools and GP surgeries to cope with the perceived increase in occupants. However, the question arises, who is eligible for the new affordable houses that are going to be built? This brings into focus how local borough councils will respond to the plans, and the response is likely to be different for each individual borough, but I can highlight the approach that WBC is taking to meet government targets.

A controversial plan for over 350 homes and a care home was granted approval in Wokingham in June 2025.[381] This approval was despite Wokingham Borough Council (WBC) refusing the project planning permission after the council received over 1000 complaints from local residents. One concern that local schools would not have sufficient capacity to cope with the influx was dismissed by the government as having no substantial evidence.[382] The problem for local councils is that they need to prove that the harm to the community significantly outweighs the benefits. In this instance, WBC failed to prove that this was the case.

WBC's flagship development is the Barkham Square, Arborfield, Wokingham Without and Hall Farm development. The plan is to develop 4500 new houses.[383] Some new homes to be occupied by people moving from outside the area. Between 35% and 50% will be affordable housing, to be made available for the children and grandchildren of Wokingham (presumably on the housing list). New housing will ensure plenty of jobs across a wide range of industries. A joint survey of the residents of Arborfield and Barkham 99% agreed

---

[381] Ruth Lucas. 350 homes and care home plans approved in Barkham approved at govt appeal. Wokingham Today. 5 June 2025.
[382] Lucas.
[383] Wokingham Borough Council Arborfield & Barkham neighbourhood plan 2019-2036. Annex VI natural environment May 2019.

that the unique identity of the area is best preserved by retaining open spaces. only 3% of the population uses buses, the diversity of destinations of residents makes it impossible to reduce the dependence on cars in favour of public transport. WBC's proposal to increase the frequency of the number 3 bus would have very little impact on transport requirements. Within the plan, there are a number of wildlife sites, copses, ancient woodland and a bluebell wood, and there are 400 locations where protected species have been recorded. Several concerns were raised, not least that the development would push traffic from the 4500 homes onto existing roads, and Planning Inspectors did express concerns about the proposal and whether it was sustainable.[384] The problem is that without a better road structure, the roads will be gridlocked, and with the woodland basis of the area, the building of such a large number of houses not only could destroy habitats but could also lead to potential flooding in the area. Therefore, the cost of the plan increases with each round of deliberation and some of the difficulties more be unsurmountable.

In a similar vein, there are 112 HMOs registered with WBC in 2025, a rise from 16 in 2018. Surprisingly, there were only four complaints regarding HMOs in 2025, and there have been no HMO licenses revoked by WBC in 2025.[385] The true impact of HMOs has not been felt in Wokingham yet, but with the likelihood of more immigrants coming to Wokingham in the near future, this may change. There are currently 345 people waiting for housing in Wokingham, but the average time waiting for a 3-bedroom property is 15.2 years.[386] It will be interesting to see how the waiting list changes once the building programme is completed. However, under a new Labour government

<hr>

[384] Guest contributor. From the opposition: Concerns over local plan. Wokingham Today. 5 May 2025.
[385] Wokingham Borough Council. Request 20110. 29 August 2025.
[386] Wokingham Borough Council. Request 20152. 28 July 2025.

scheme, which over 200 councils have expressed an interest in, new council houses are being built for illegal migrants while local families are stuck on the waiting lists.[387]

Businesses

Like a number of high streets and town centres up and down the country, Wokingham has lost a number of long-standing shops as well as new shops that have been unable to continue trading.[388] Wokingham has been subject to the loss of department stores, which at the height of the crisis saw up to fifty shop closures per week.[389] The knock-on effect of the loss of retail jobs, which drives unemployment in the town, is of concern. The demise of shops is blamed on a number of factors, such as parking charges and business rates imposed by the central government, which have a major impact on what is occurring on high streets across the country. Local councillors in Wokingham claimed that a Labour government would provide the support that businesses need to improve shopping areas within Wokingham, but in reality, the Labour government has added to the problem rather than solved it.[390]

It is clear that high street shops are diminishing across the country, and the problem isn't specific to Wokingham. This has become a considerable worry for voters up and down the country, but principally among Reform UK voters and supporters.[391] It is forecast that labour is threatened with annihilation at the next general election unless it

---

[387] David Bull Reform UK. Facebook item, January 2026.
[388] Marie-Louise Weighill. From the chamber: Empty shop fronts darken town like lost teeth. Wokingham Today. 24 February 2024.
[389] Marie-Louise Weighill.
[390] Marie-Louise Weighill.
[391] Michael Goodier, Josh Halliday. Labour risks election wipeout unless it improves Brittain's high streets, study finds. The Guardian 28 January 2026.

resolves the decline of the UK's shopping centres, especially given that there are eight thousand fewer retail stores in 2025 compared with 2019.[392] Higher national insurance contributions for employers and higher business rates introduced by Rachel Reeves are the main drivers in the decline of retail stores on Britain's high streets.

This can be seen through the shocking revelations that show more than 6,000 bank and building society high street branches have closed since 2015, or are due to close by the end of 2025. Approximately 5,000 Main Street banks remain open. In Wokingham, Santander, Barclays, NatWest and Lloyds have all closed branches in the last two years.[393] Southern Co-op has closed its branch in Wokingham, which added to efflux of shops and the further decline of Wokingham's main shopping centre.[394] What hurts residents the most is when prominent independent traders cease trading, and the main reason for the closure of Phil's Good Food store was the hostile car parking charges imposed by the Lib Dem council, which has kept shoppers out of the centre of Wokingham.[395] The closure of this independent trader provoked an angry reaction from residents that Wokingham is losing everything and reiterated concern for the future of the town.[396] Indeed, there were pleas for Wokingham council to wake up as four businesses closed in the town centre in three weeks.[397] The children's clothes shop Little Piggy is closing and leaving Wokingham, citing a 35 percent increase in rent and the extensive road works that affected footfall in the town

---

[392] Goodier, Halliday.

[393] Giles Sheldrick. Reform UK unveils nine-point plan to rejuvenate Britain's barren high streets. The Express, 3 March 2025.

[394] Andrew Batt. Co-op in Wokingham announces closure, while new business is set to come to town. Wokingham Today, 14 January 2026.

[395] Andrew Batt. Another business falls: Independent Wokingham food shop shuts its doors. Wokingham Today. 20 January 2026.

[396] Staff writer. 'We're losing everything we love': Closure of Wokingham shop sparks fears for town's future. Wokingham Today, 21 January 2026.

[397] Staff writer. 'Wake up, Wokingham council': Fourth business closure in just three weeks. Wokingham Today. 29 January 2026.

as the main reasons to relocate. Residents believe that the town is being choked to death by the local Lib Dem council.

Britain's high streets are slipping into a state of oblivion, with residents in towns across the country protesting that their dying shopping centres are devoid and are alert to an absence of social unity is on the increase.[398] There is a clear requirement for more support and investment if local shopping centres are going to reverse the decline. Most of the policies currently contemplated to address the problems facing our high streets concentrate on tackling the visual, noticeable signals of a local drop in numbers of shops, and rejuvenating the high street sustainability to ensure that they thrive again.[399] There is an obvious need to stimulate high streets and encourage growth, and this requires creating the conditions for businesses to thrive there and for consumers to spend their money.[400] In this regard, Reform UK have come up with a nine-point plan to help reinvigorate local high streets, which includes introducing time-limited free parking and abolishing the high parking charges introduced by many councils, including those imposed in Wokingham.[401] Make the streets cleaner and introduce more visible policing so that women and children feel safer in town centres. Shift the tax burden to prosperous online shopping retailers and businesses, and scrap business rates for small businesses to encourage investment in the high street.[402] Lift the minimum profit threshold for corporation tax and give entrepreneurs the breathing space they need in the first few years to get their operations off the ground. Also, councils and HMRC can assist in encouraging

---

[398] George Bunn. Decline of Britain's high streets exposed as residents tell GB news funding vow is just another Labour gimmick. GB News 10 October 2025.

[399] Jessica Craig. The government needs a new high street strategy. Here's what they should do. Power to Change. 29 January 2026.

[400] Jessica Craig.

[401] Giles Sheldrick. Reform UK unveils nine-point plan to rejuvenate Britain's barren high streets. The Express 3 March 2025.

[402] Giles Sheldrick.

businesses, retailers and entrepreneurs to invest in local high streets by simply phoning around to encourage investment.[403] There is a cost to this plan; however, shops that have closed down don't contribute any tax to the council, and there are no employees to pay income tax and make national insurance contributions.[404]

Council Tax Waste

Wokingham Borough Council have identified the requirement of setting a prudent budget that matches expenditure with income.[405] It is important to support those most in need in our community, especially children and adults with disabilities, learning difficulties, those with mental health problems and the elderly. However, there have been cuts to these services without explanation, with several schemes stopped or discontinued in December 2025 without any explanation to the recipients of these council-supported schemes. This is despite the promise by the Lib Dem council that they would engage and consult people on how the council needs to respond to budget constraints.[406] We have already covered the expensive and meaningless costs of the solar panel farms, which could easily cover the shortfall in funding. The council recognised there would be a shortfall in funding ahead and

---

[403] Giles Sheldrick.

[404] Giles Sheldrick.

[405] Wokingham Borough Council. Budget 2025/26: Cantley parking charges won't be introduced. 12 February 2025.

[406] Wokingham Borough Council. Budget 2025/26.

that they would have to make tough decisions.[407] This would leave WBC with challenging decisions on spending on income generation.[408]

Furthermore, this raises the question of why the Lib Dem council went ahead and pushed to make Wokingham a preferred centre for migrants, knowing that these people would have no source of income, would require much sought-after council housing and would compete with our young people for the few jobs that remain vacant within Wokingham. New research has uncovered that council spending across the country has risen by £83 million in five years.[409] The surge in spending corresponds with the continued influx of illegal immigrants. The overall cost for asylum-associated social care for both children and adults has exceeded doubling to £744 million in a five-year period. No wonder there is a shortfall in funds in many councils across Britain. The Labour government claim they do not recognise these numbers.[410] Therefore, the question arises, where is all the council overspending coming from? I suspect from a lot of different areas.

It is clear that the Lib Dem-run WBC is far from efficient and is wasteful in its spending. The Carnival Pool flats project has been disastrous, with an estimated loss of £2.7 million according to opposition parties.[411] Another £1 million pounds by the flawed design work on the Toutley East project, and £600,000 wasted on empty offices in the Shute End headquarters. Should Reform UK win seats on the WBC in the upcoming elections in May 2026, then we will be

---

[407] Andrew Batt. "Tough decisions" ahead as Wokingham Borough Council could be forced to find millions in savings. Wokingham Today, 24 July 2025.

[408] Stephen Conway. From the leader: Wokingham's local plan update. Wokingham Today, 11 January 2026.

[409] Charles Hymas. Council spending on migrant social care rises by £83m in five years. The Telegraph, 1 February 2026.

[410] Charles Hymas.

[411] Wokingham Matters Latest news from Wokingham Conservatives, winter 2025/26.

in a much better position to investigate and reveal the true extent of council tax mismanagement. Reform UK has already called into question the exuberant council tax rises being proposed by other councils.[412]

Reform UK councils have saved taxpayers millions of pounds sterling by scrapping net zero and have saved up to £50 million by cutting or stopping other wasteful costs.[413] One area where UK councils have been able to save money is through unmasking illegal houses of multiple occupancy, and landlords must now apply for a licence or face a number of fines up to £30,000. Richard Tice claims that Reform UK councils have saved taxpayers £331 million in six months.[414] The savings come through Reform UK's Department of Government Efficiency, commonly called DOGE. The savings have been achieved by stopping wasteful schemes and by cutting green policies. Savings have been made by improving digital services, by selling unused land and by renegotiating debts. The biggest savings appear to be coming from slashing wasteful net-zero policies.[415] Reform UK has promised to fix broken Britain. However, it is not all plain sailing for Reform UK councillors, as a Worcestershire County councillor quit the party over plans to raise council tax above the 4.99 percent current limit.[416]

---

[412] Dorset View. Reform calls Bournemouth council tax rises 'madness.' 23 January 2026.

[413] Daniel Martin. Reform councils 'save taxpayers £40m' by scrapping net zero. The Telegraph. 7 August 2025.

[414] BritBrief.co.uk. Reform councils save taxpayers £331m in six months, claims Tice. 16 November 2025.

[415] Daniel Martin. Reform councils save UK taxpayers millions by slashing wasteful net zero policies. Climatechangedispatch, 8 August 2025.

[416] Dominic Penna. Reform councillor quits party on live TV over council tax raid. The Telegraph, 8 February 2026.

What Is Missing: A Personal View

I agree wholeheartedly with David Goodhart when he states that 'For several years now more than half of British people have agreed with the statement (and similar ones): In recent years Britain has changed beyond recognition, it now resembles a foreign country which makes me feel uncomfortable.'[417] Goodhart states that this view is particularly held by older, well-educated and the least affluent, of which I am a paid-up member. I couldn't have envisaged the changes to Britain 12 years ago. Today, things are moving at an alarming rate and appear totally out of control, and it is easy to see that Britain is broken. The question is it broken beyond repair? The only political party looking to repair Britain is Reform UK, and it has a monumental task to repair the damage. I don't understand why the Lib Dems and many Labour MPs want closer ties with the EU. To me, to me, it is mind-boggling stupid. Their arguments for rejoining the EU and disregarding the democratic will of the people are even more foolish. I want to live in a country that has self-rule and is not answerable to outside forces. I do not want to live in a country that has surrendered its sovereignty to Brussels. I want to see the NHS restored, with waiting lists coming down and more GPs and GP practices opened to meet the demand. I want to see British people who have been on waiting lists for housing given preference over people coming into the country either legally or in small boats. I want to see more houses built, but with realistic goals that are attainable and not some made-up, farcical dream.

I don't want to live in a country where multiculturalism is normal because multiculturalism doesn't work inasmuch as immigrants will always congregate with people that they identify with, and they demand

---

[417] David Goodhart. The road to somewhere: The new tribes shaping British politics, page 2-3. Penguin Random House, Londo, UK. 2017.

their culture replace the British culture and that the British people pay for their demands. As Goodhart stated, when he interviewed young Asians in the mill towns of the north, he found that they mostly had no white friends until they went to college, and they held bizarre views of British society.[418] I don't think it is racist to want to see the country and government put the interests of British people before the interests of immigrants. I don't believe it is wrong to want to be safe in our own country, nor to see that our children are free from being intimidated by foreigners. I want to see our prisons emptied of foreign prisoners who are deported back to their own countries. As Goodhart eloquently stated, "One appealing definition of a well-integrated society is one in which everyone is a potential friend."[419] This would be a society that is moving towards utopia and is, in reality, beyond what could be achieved in the UK under the current climate. The more choices people are given, the more likely there will be ethnic clustering because people will congregate in places where they feel safe and with others they can identify with.[420] I'm not against asylum seekers coming to Britain if they apply through the proper channels and are vetted as coming because they are escaping tyranny and not fleeing from justice in the home countries or they are coming to destroy British values. I would like to see leaders in the established churches working to help integrate asylum seekers into our communities as valued members, as I believe it is the only way to prevent the ghettoes that we are witnessing across Britain. In our communities everyone should be valued as a friend not be held in suspicion of their motives for being here. People who will integrate into society and make a meaningful contribution through employment.

I want to see justice for British girls who were raped by rape gangs, and I want to see MPs who have covered up the rape gang problem

---

[418] Goodhart, page 127.
[419] Goodhart, page 128.
[420] Goodhart, page 128.

prosecuted and put in prison. I would like to see the death penalty reintroduced for anyone who has raped a child less than 12 years of age. I would like to see more apprenticeships and career paths for young people between the ages of 16 and 25 years to give them hope and a future. I would like to see incentives for British industry to grow, as industry is the bedrock of growth and the stability of the country.[421] The GDP statistics show that imported cheap labour does not improve Britain's GDP; it subtracts from it, while industrial growth will improve GDP and the standards of living for everyone. I want to live in a country where hard-working people are rewarded for their efforts and not taxed almost out of existence. I would like to see the incentives for staying on benefits and not working removed. I want to see Britain return to looking after the elderly, for they are the people who have brought Britain this far. I would like to live in a Britain where everyone is valued regardless of academic ability, ethnicity, gender, or social background. A Britain where people are free to express their views without threatening, violent or insulting behaviour.

I want to see Christian values restored, where children are taught about men and women and are not penalised for being patriotic. I would like to see British history taught in schools and children taught to be proud of their country. I want to be able to go to my local pub without fear of it being closed down due to the inappropriate greed of the government. I want an end to wasteful net zero spending and it being replaced by investment in innovative schemes that will reduce the carbon footprint and reduce greenhouse gases. I want to be able to take a walk in the countryside and see trees and wildlife, not miles of solar panels. I want to see the end of members of parliament who claim to love the country but then do everything they can to destroy it. I

---

[421] Goodhart, page 177.

would like to see a change in the law that only those born in Britain can stand to represent Britain in parliament and local government.

It is one thing for Reform UK to be ahead in every single poll in over a year, on many occasions by over 10 points, but it is quite another to turn that lead into seats in Westminster. So many of us desperately want to see Nigel Farage as our next Prime Minister, leading a Reform UK government, but we need to turn our vision into reality. Remember, at the 2024 election, Reform UK had more votes than the Lib Dems, but we had five seats in Westminster while the Lib Dems had 72 seats.

My final thought is that I would like to see a Britain where good triumphs over evil, where justice is done, where everyone is valued and where people have an improved standard of living across all walks of life. Reform UK, family, community and country. These values and visions are shared by many others across our country. We are not the far-right, we are the centre normal. We move forward with optimism and hope for the local council elections in May 2026.

Other Books Available

The book explores seven key areas of the victorious Christian life and remaining free in Christ regardless of the circumstances we find ourselves facing in the coming days. As Christians, we are either afraid of or want to skip over quickly the challenging teachings in the word of God, such as the struggles with and consequences of sin, and the coming wrath of God, in order to reach the more positive teachings on salvation and eternal life for all who believe in Jesus as Lord and Saviour.

All of us want to be free from the things that hold us captive in life. Jesus offered us the opportunity to know the truth, and that his truth would set us free. Totally free means being set free to be the person God created us to be, to be free from fear, from circumstances, from the strongholds that tell us that we can never achieve all that we want to achieve. The Bible is the only source of the truth that promises to set us free. This book explores the principles and defines the tenets that allow us to be set free from the strongholds that bind us and try to limit us to less than we are capable of achieving in this life. The book outlines some of the major obstacles that bind us and stop us from being free. The book also indicates how we can find the freedom that Jesus promised through the truth of the Gospel. The book explores twelve areas of the truth of the Christian life and outlines some of the principles needed to remain free in Christ, regardless of the circumstances we find ourselves facing.

The book provides an overview of who God is and why we can rely upon him regardless of the circumstances we find ourselves facing. A clearer understanding of the living God and his awesome power to deliver and rescue us from a world that is out of control, and becoming darker as we move towards the end of this age, will help us all to stand firm and know that God has plans for each of us. Those plans will give hope and a future and show that God's ultimate purpose is to bring us into a closer, more profound and deeper relationship with him.

There is a lot of talk and discussion in these last days about what all religions have in common, and can this common ground be exploited to make a single religion? Indeed, there have been conferences to discuss how this can be achieved to bring Christianity under a single umbrella. However, in order to do this, everything must be removed from Christianity that is offensive to other religions. Therefore, it is more important than ever to reiterate what is unique to our Christian beliefs and, above all else, that Jesus Christ is our Lord and Saviour. There is no other name in heaven by which we may be saved from the coming anger of God. We have received the Spirit of God so that we may know what God has freely given to us. Christ crucified is a stumbling block to the Jews and foolishness to all those who have not entered the Kingdom of God. In this book, I have outlined and discussed the uniqueness of Christ and expounded on God's purposes for His Kingdom on the earth in the last days of this age and on His Kingdom in the world to come. I have also shown who we are in Christ and have reminded us that we are God's treasured possession.